# Praise for the Book

"*'Self-Defense for Massage Therapists' is a valuable resource for both new and experienced massage therapists. In our profession, we focus on providing quality care while respecting client boundaries. Unfortunately, we don't always anticipate situations where clients may challenge or violate our own boundaries, but it does happen. This book offers meaningful insight into preventing inappropriate behavior through effective communication, body language, and professionalism. It also equips therapists with the tools and mindset needed to respond when boundaries are crossed. Whether working in a clinic, visiting a client's home, or entering a hotel room, therapists must stay aware of their surroundings and be prepared to recognize potential danger. Teresa clearly outlines self-defense techniques that massage therapists can use with confidence and precision to protect themselves. I believe this information is essential, not only to be read but also practiced. I highly recommend participating in the hands-on course to ensure therapists feel both confident and competent in applying these techniques in real-life situations.*"

**—Donna Sarvello, MBA, LMT**

*"Preparation can be the difference between feeling safe or victimized. May you be blessed to never have to use the wisdom that has been so delicately submitted into this book. However, in situations of ethical transference, power differential, and misconstrued intentions, stating your purposes clearly is crucial, and if that does not work, make them known palpably. I have been a massage therapy instructor for many years as a teacher of ethics. I have mentored massage therapists through situations that have not been comfortable. If they had prepared by understanding the power they have and how to manage the room, many of the offensive behaviors would never have happened. Thank you for reading this book and building your confidence in your body, mind, and strength."*

**—Nathan Nordstrom LMT BCTMB**
**Director of Training and Massage**
**Therapy Industry Relations**
**Hand & Stone Massage and Facial Corp.**

*"This is a great read for all 'hands-on' professions (massage, nursing, CNA, PT, OT, etc.). The information in this book is so important and should be taught, not just at the beginning of the program but also throughout the program, using all of the scenarios to engage students to discuss what they would do if found in the situations. As instructors, we have an obligation to get this information out to our students! We don't want to wait for an incident to happen... Have them PREPARED, AWARE, AND READY for ANY situation. This book covers it all!"*

**—Jody Stork**
**Space Coast Education Center**

*"Written by my teacher of over twenty-five years, this book is a powerful extension of what she first taught me during massage school two decades ago. Even then, she emphasized the importance of professional boundaries and how to navigate inappropriate advances with clarity and strength. This education allowed me to grow my successful massage and spa establishment into an ethical and respectful business. Now, Teresa and her son, Johnny, have shared that same wisdom in this essential guide for all massage therapists and healthcare professionals. With compassion and experience, they offer practical tools to protect both practitioners and clients. I consider this book a must-read for anyone in the healing profession committed to having a safe, ethical practice."*

**—Carla Morello**
**Shine Massage and Spa Wellness**

*"Teresa Matthews delivers an essential, empowering guide with Self-Defense for Massage Therapists. Drawing on decades of experience in martial arts, bodywork, and personal safety, Teresa and Johnny equip therapists with the tools to stay safe, confident, and in control—both in and out of the treatment room. This book blends powerful, real-world stories, practical exercises, and clear instructions to tackle one of the profession's most overlooked risks: personal vulnerability. From setting firm boundaries to executing effective self-defense techniques, every chapter is a masterclass in proactive protection. This is not just a manual—it's a movement toward safety, self-awareness, and strengthening our profession."*

**—Drew Freedman, Founder**
**The Boston Bodyworker, Learn2Tape®**

# Self-Defense for Massage Therapists

## A Practical Guide to Prevent Unacceptable Behaviors and Habits to Empower Your Personal Safety

**Teresa M. Matthews &**
**Johnny R. Matthews**

Global Book
Publishing

ISBN: 978-1-964644-33-2
Book Design & Publishing done by:
Global Book Publishing
www.globalbookpublishing.com

## DISCLAIMER STATEMENT

This book aims to provide information on self-defense. It is not the purpose of this manual to reprint all the information that is otherwise available about self-defense and martial arts, but to complement, amplify, and supplement other texts. You are urged to read all the available material, educate yourself as much as possible about self-defense, and tailor the information to your individual needs. Every effort has been made to make this manual as complete and accurate as possible. This text should be used only as a general guide and not as the ultimate source of self-defense information.

Furthermore, this manual contains information on self-defense that is current only up to the printing date. This manual's purpose is to help educate and entertain.

The information, stories, and articles in this book are the opinions of the authors based on their personal observations and years of experience. Neither the authors nor the publisher assumes any liability whatsoever for the use of or inability to use any or all information present in this publication.

All participants must take all responsibility to ensure they are free from any medical condition that could contraindicate taking part in any form of movement and exercise.

The publishers and authors of this book are confident that when properly performed, the exercises are safe.

This book serves as a reference to enhance personal safety.

*Thank you Kimberly Matthews*
*(my daughter-in-law) for lovely photos*
*in the book*

# Table of Contents

# Foreword

Teresa Matthews has masterfully blended her extensive expertise in Taekwondo and police tactics into this essential guide for personal protection and self-care. In a world where the unexpected can occur at any moment, Matthews equips readers with the knowledge and skills necessary to prevent unwanted behaviors and protect themselves.

This book not only teaches practical self-defense techniques but also highlights the importance of situational awareness, confidence, and safety in both professional and personal settings. From understanding how to read body language and scan for potential threats to learning how to escape dangerous situations, Matthews provides a comprehensive framework that empowers individuals to take control of their own safety.

Each chapter includes real-life scenarios, expert insights, and practical exercises that will prepare readers to handle a wide range of threats with confidence. Whether you are new to self-defense or looking to enhance your existing skills, this book offers clear, actionable strategies for staying safe.

Matthews also emphasizes the importance of self-care, encouraging readers to build physical endurance, strength, and balance to be prepared not only to defend themselves but also to maintain a healthy lifestyle. This is more than just a book—it's a roadmap to protecting your body, mind, and spirit in an ever-changing world.

Charles W. Coker, 9th Dan
Grandmaster & Founder
Yesha TaeKwonDo
www.yeshatkd.org

# Preface

Growing up with three older brothers, they taught me to fight and defend myself. Whether it was how to throw a punch, palm heal strike, kick, or wrestle (my brother Ronnie was an all-state wrestler), they taught me to do whatever it takes to win—or get away and stay safe. These values and my upbringing eventually ended up creating the groundwork for this book.

When I was in High School, my favorite subject was gym class! I remember one day in gym class, we had a self-defense demonstration. That, to me, was the best class EVER! To be able to use our bodies in a way to stay safe, ward off a bad guy and not really have to be crazy super strong to do so sounded unbelievable and amazing! Having the ability to use leverage and momentum to get away from a bad situation simply brought out this passion in me.

When I first started my martial arts career, the very first day my sensei said, "We learn and train in Self-Defense to know how to use it. The true art of Self-Defense is NEVER having to use it." That's why my goal is to open your eyes to what could be a potential issue and to have the ability to avoid that unacceptable behavior in any circumstance.

Together, my son Johnny and I have created this book to share why you should set personal boundaries to protect yourself from unacceptable behavior! This guide is geared toward massage therapists and other healthcare professionals, but it is also designed for your family and friends to use in daily life.

Through our years of teaching, many healthcare professionals have shared scenarios with us that they have encountered in their treatment room. It was an eye-opener.

So, why have I NEVER had any unacceptable behavior from a client? Let me tell you what I do and why I have stayed safe. I wish to educate you, inspire you and even challenge you to follow my lead!

Again, I will always remember the words from my Sensei. Self-defense is not about fighting. It is about knowing how NOT to get into a fight.

# How This Book Came About

When my son, Johnny (a police officer), went back to the academy to become a Defensive Tactic Instructor with the Police Force, I was curious and looked through his textbook. As I did, I saw many parallels between how the police train to how I have handled myself in life and especially in my profession as a Licensed Massage Therapist. That is where it all began!

Massage therapists are generally in a 10' × 12' room with a stranger, a client they have seen multiple times, or someone they know. In any case, I have been very fortunate to NEVER have a client (male or female) touch me inappropriately. Why is that?? What do I do that makes my client abstain from doing anything inappropriate? Johnny and I discussed this and realized other therapists need to understand what we knew. To do that, our course "Protecting Your Assets: Self-Defense for the Health Care Professional" came to life in 2015.

We had no idea what would come out of the teachings. To our shock, we had many therapists come forward and share their situations they went through with a client. They gave us permission to share those situations in the chapters to come.

In our classes, we had so many people say, "I wish I knew this in school!" That created our mission… we want all students, therapists, and all healthcare professionals to get this knowledge! Even though we geared our program to healthcare professionals, we have also had many therapists bring their friends, family members, and even teenagers to our class, and they all left wanting more!

So, here is your "MORE"!

# How to Effectively Use This Book

In the following chapters, we will share real stories and situations that have put therapists in a very uncomfortable situation and ask you how you would have handled those situations if you were the "victim." If you have children, you teach them not to talk to strangers or take candy from strangers because you want to keep them safe. We may have to give them reminders. Please keep in mind that we are not trying to scare you or put fear in you. We want to let you know that there are people who may try to do unacceptable things.

As you read this book, you will be able to put all the pieces together. There will be tactical tools to avoid an unwanted, unacceptable situation. There will also be tools to help you "fight for your life" if it comes to that. You should read this book or portions of this book more than once to keep the information fresh in your mind and give yourself reminders. The goal of this book is to keep you safe in and out of the treatment room.

In order to handle yourself when with someone who makes you uncomfortable, you will need to understand there are several habits and tools you need to keep yourself safe and prepared to prevent unwanted behavior.

We encourage you to share this information with your friends, family, children, and colleagues, so they also may learn to stay safe and defend themselves.

CHAPTER 1

# Protecting Your Assets

What comes to mind when you read the words "Protecting Your Assets?" Do you think about your financial protection? Most do, but besides financial protection, what other assets should we be protecting?

Yes, we need to protect our financial accounts—by having strong passwords that could deter someone from hacking our accounts. Besides our financial accounts, we have many other assets we need to protect—our home, car, sporting equipment, musical instruments, furniture, pets, plants, phone, and, of course, children and family members. What we also NEED to add to this list is US! Our physical body needs to be the biggest asset we protect.

We don't want to live in constant fear of things and circumstances such as... "OMG, what if someone makes me get into a car accident while I'm driving to work?" We don't think about situations to live in fear, so we have got to take precautions in order to be safe. When driving to and from work, we may drive defensively not to get in an accident by paying attention to our surroundings. This mentality is exactly what we need when we are out in public or in a treatment room with a client.

The question is, "How do we protect these assets?" There are many of the listed assets we have learned to protect without too much thought because we know what the outcome could be if we did not prepare with adequate protection. We have habits we practice daily that help keep those assets protected. It's all around us on a daily basis! We also want to remember that we need to PREPARE in order to PROTECT.

Some examples of how we protect our assets: For our home, we lock the doors, have cameras, ring doorbell camera, security system, hoping to prevent a robber from entering our home; for our car, we have a backup camera to prevent us from hitting anything; in our bathroom, we put a rubber mat down in the shower not to slip and fall or a grab bar to hold on to prevent us from falling and getting hurt; and all of us apply sunblock on our skin when we go outside to prevent getting sunburn. It makes sense to be prepared for the worst. For example, we prepare our pantry with enough items if we are expecting extreme weather and a power outage. Without electricity, life will change in an instant.

Don't panic. If your emergency preparedness plan has a few holes in it right now, you're in the right place.

Are you prepared if the power goes out? Do you have candles for light? How are you going to stay cool or warm? How are you going to cook?

Here is a display to be prepared for a hurricane:

We are told to be prepared and stay safe, so we plan ahead before the hurricane even gets to us. I think you are getting the idea. We do things just in case something "could" happen. **We plan to prevent and protect!**

**Being prepared is about more than stocking up. It's about thinking creatively and learning essential survival skills.**

*Boy Scout Motto: BE PREPARED!!*

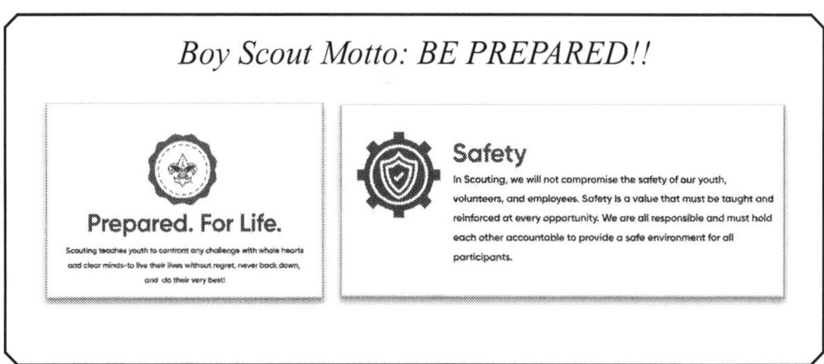

Working with clients in a private room, sadly, many colleagues have shared stories of being touched inappropriately. They did not expect any of these situations to occur. Healthcare professionals focus on helping people heal, so the idea of their client doing something inappropriately doesn't even cross their minds. What could they have done to prevent these situations? Could they have prepared in advance to stay safe? Throughout this book, I will share those stories with you and ask you, "What would you do?".

The following chapters will give you the tools to protect yourself from unwanted, aggressive behavior. Get ready to prepare well!

**What would you do?**

*Paul treated a female client with back pain. He worked on her back with her prone, then side lying for about twenty minutes. When he turned her supine, she grabbed his hand and placed it between her legs.*

*Find out what Paul did in Chapter 10.*

CHAPTER 2

# Introduction to Self-Defense

As mentioned in the Preface, self-defense is knowing what to do if we have to defend ourselves, but the true art is NOT having to use it.

Self-defense refers to the legal right to protect oneself from harm. It may involve using reasonable force to prevent an imminent threat or attack. The concept varies by jurisdiction, but generally, it allows individuals to defend themselves against physical harm, provided their response is proportional to the threat. This can include physical techniques but also includes nonviolent measures, like escaping a dangerous situation.

Understanding self-defense involves grasping its principles, legal context, and practical applications. Here's a breakdown:

- **Self-defense:** The act of protecting oneself from harm or imminent danger. This can involve physical actions, along with verbal de-escalation.
- **Justifiable force:** Self-defense is usually justified when there is an immediate threat. Laws vary by location, so

it's important to know your local regulations regarding the use of force. Is the danger immediate or can you avoid it?

- **Proportionality:** The response must be proportional to the threat. For example, using deadly force in response to a minor threat may not be justified. The level of force used in self-defense must be reasonable and not excessive compared to the threat.
- **Reasonable belief:** The person defending themselves must have a reasonable belief that they are in danger.
- **Duty to retreat:** Some jurisdictions require individuals to retreat from danger, if safely possible, before resorting to force.
- **Physical self-defense:** One can use techniques from martial arts, boxing, or other combat sports.
- **Verbal self-defense:** De-escalation strategies are used to defuse potentially dangerous situations.
- **Preventive:** Awareness and avoidance tactics are in play to stay out of harmful situations.
- **Situational awareness:** Pay attention to your surroundings and trust your instincts.
- **Conflict resolution:** Consider how you can avoid conflicts and handle situations nonviolently.

By understanding these components, you can gain a well-rounded perspective on self-defense, its importance, and how to protect yourself effectively.

Self-defense is also about being aware of your surroundings and recognizing a possible threat. Understanding the skills necessary to control an uncomfortable situation and remain safe is the ultimate goal. We want to achieve an optimal outcome from a complex situation.

## De-Escalate a Situation/Threat Assessment

De-escalating conflict is a way to reduce tension and disagreement between people. It's an important skill that can help prevent conflicts from escalating into more serious issues. When we can de-escalate an uncomfortable situation, we can avoid a physical conflict.

Here are some tips for "verbally" de-escalating a conflict:

- **Remain calm:** Try to stay calm and regulated, even if you're feeling angry or upset. If you need to, take a step back and take some deep breaths. Do not raise your voice.
- **Be respectful:** Treat others with dignity and respect, and avoid using offensive language or gestures.
- **Listen actively:** Give the other person your full attention, nod, ask questions, and avoid interrupting or changing the subject. Active listening can help you show respect, understand their perspective, and acknowledge their feelings.
- **Empathize:** Show genuine concern and a willingness to understand without judging. Speaking calmly can also help show empathy.

- **Validate feelings:** Showing that the other person's feelings are important and legitimate can help de-escalate conflict and make both parties more receptive to each other's point of view.
- **Apologize sincerely:** If you're apologizing for a mistake or inconvenience, take responsibility, express regret, and offer a solution.

What if someone is physically coming toward you? How do we de-escalate a person physically? If we know the optimal thing is to escape and remove ourselves from the situation, we can use their momentum to our advantage.

"Physical de-escalation" refers to techniques used to calm a tense or potentially violent situation without resorting to physical force. Here are some tips:

- **Stay calm:** Your demeanor can influence the situation. Maintain a steady voice and relaxed body language.
- **Create space:** Give the person some physical space. Being too close can feel threatening.
- **Nonthreatening posture:** Avoid crossed arms and aggressive stances. Keep open hands and a relaxed posture.
- **Active listening:** Show you're listening by nodding and using verbal affirmations. Repeat back what they say to show understanding.
- **Use a soft tone:** Speak in a calm and considerate voice. A lower volume can help diffuse tension.

- **Empathize:** Acknowledge their feelings. Phrases like "I can see you're upset" can validate their emotions.
- **Offer choices:** Empower the person by giving them options. This can help them feel in control.
- **Keep your distance:** Maintain a safe distance to reduce feelings of intimidation.
- **Be mindful of your surroundings:** Position yourself near an exit in case you need to leave quickly.
- **Use distraction:** Shift focus to another topic or activity to redirect their energy.
- **Know when to walk away:** If the situation escalates, it may be best to remove yourself and seek help.

If the situation escalates, and the person comes close to us, we need to get ourselves to a safer place. Here is a demonstration of using their momentum to our advantage.

We swing one leg behind us and use both arms to push them at their shoulder and away from us. As we do, we allow ourselves to move in the opposite direction, making us able to escape the area.

In a later chapter, we will show other physical engagements, such as joint manipulations. (We discuss it more in Chapter 7.)

The following picture shows how we can pivot our back leg behind us and put our hands on their shoulder. This allows us to create an angle for them to be pushed away from us and we use this force to get ourselves to escape.

# Redirection Technique

To begin, we look at the person approaching us in a "Ready Stance." A ready stance is a balanced and symmetrical position that prepares you to quickly and efficiently react to a situation, whether in martial arts, sports, or other contexts. Our hands are up in order to react quickly.

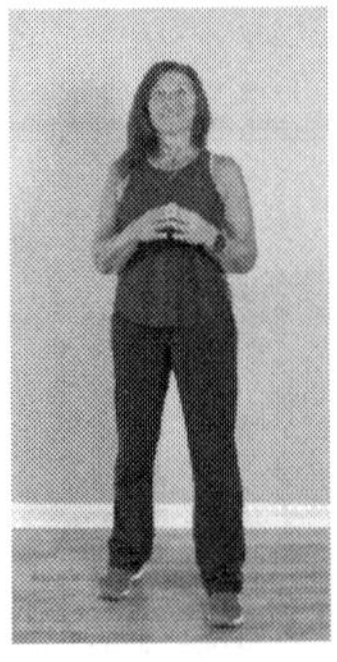

*Ready stance*

*Redirection technique*

**What would you do?**

*Cheryl worked on a male client four times over a three-month period. Everything was just fine, until his fifth visit. She completed the session and told the male client to take his time getting up and come out of the room when he was ready. As she was walking out the door, he grabbed her arm and pulled her close to him, and kissed her.*

*Find out what Cheryl did in Chapter 10.*

CHAPTER 3

# Confidence

Confidence is hard to define, but self-confidence refers to a sense of comfort with yourself and your instincts and a belief that you can trust your own abilities, knowledge, and judgment.

Everyone can view confidence differently. What makes us confident? Is it the way we dress, act, look, perform, or something else? Recently, when talking with a friend who is the lead singer in a band, I complimented him on his haircut. His response was perfect, "Once I cut my hair, I felt more confident!" A haircut can have a big impact on confidence. Changing your hairstyle can help you feel refreshed and more aligned with how you want to present yourself. It can also boost your self-image, especially if it enhances your features or matches your personal style. Plus, the act of taking time for self-care can contribute to feeling more confident overall. So, yes, the way we look is one way that affects our confidence.

## Project Confidence

We do best when we have confidence in all aspects of our life. Think about your job/career/profession. Do you speak in a confident, strong manner? Without being too aggressive or overpowering, are you able to speak and control a situation? This is all achieved with confidence.

Building self-confidence promotes personal growth that positively influences both your professional and personal life. In this chapter, we will discuss many ways to gain confidence.

## Verbal Confidence

- **Practice regularly:** Improve your speaking skills in regular conversations with friends and family, or in groups.
- **Know your material:** When speaking about a topic or presenting an idea, being knowledgeable boosts your confidence.
- **Positive self-talk:** Replace negative thoughts with positive affirmations. Remind yourself of your strengths and successes.
- **Body language:** Maintain good posture, make eye contact, and use gestures. Confident body language can enhance your verbal confidence.
- **Slow down:** Take your time while speaking. Pausing can help you gather your thoughts and sound more composed.
- **Be loud and clear:** Your voice will dictate your authority.

Think about someone you know who portrays confidence. You may say they have a certain vibe about them—you know the type—they walk in a room and it feels like they own the place, or when they go to work, they walk into the building knowing exactly where to go and that they belong there. Such people's trust, knowledge, and intuition give them the ability to project strength on their surroundings and the people around them.

Confidence isn't about being perfect. It's about being comfortable with who you are and knowing that you're valuable, just as you are.

- **Take risks:** Confident people are less afraid to step out of their comfort zone. They know that to grow, they have to try new things, even if it means they might not succeed every time.
- **Be optimistic:** Confident people are more positive and expect good things to happen. Even when things go wrong, they can see those experiences and even failures as a chance to learn and get better.
- **Accept compliments:** When someone says, "Hey, great job," a confident person has an easier time saying, "Thank you," instead of shrugging it off. They are not bragging—they just know their worth.
- **Be decisive:** Confident people find it easier to make decisions and stick to them. They trust their instincts and don't waste time worrying about what everyone else might think.
- **Set boundaries:** Knowing when to say "yes" and when to say "no" is a sign of confidence. Confident

people can respect their own limits and aren't afraid to communicate them to others.

- **Be yourself:** Confident people are more comfortable being who they are and don't feel the need to pretend to be someone they're not.
- **They listen more than they speak:** Surprisingly, confident people often listen more than they talk. They're secure enough to know they don't always have to be the loudest voice in the room.

## Are Self-Confidence and Self-Esteem the Same?

We often use self-confidence and self-esteem interchangeably because they're closely related. Self-confidence is most genuine and durable when it derives from healthy self-esteem. While they share similarities, there are distinct differences between the two.

Self-confidence is outward-facing. It's what you put out to the world and what people around you see. Self-esteem is inward-facing and only sometimes noticeable from the outside. Your confidence can come from knowledge and experience, whereas self-esteem is more about knowing yourself and valuing your self-worth.

Low self-confidence or low self-esteem can cause self-doubt, unhealthy self-talk, and negatively affect your mental health, well-being, and performance.

It's crucial to note that self-confidence won't endure without healthy self-esteem. Unfamiliar terrain will shake it. But with both, you'll thrive. When your self-esteem is steady and your well-being is good, your self-confidence shines brighter.

Love and value yourself; you'll embrace your strengths and weaknesses in any situation, and your self-esteem will motivate you to be a more confident person.

Everyone can learn how to be more confident in different, powerful ways. What may work for some may not work for all, and that's okay. Remember that you can always start small with little steps before taking bold strides.

Here are some ways to help build self-confidence:

- Stop comparing yourself to others
- Celebrate and reflect on your wins
- Embrace your failures and view them as learning opportunities
- Step out of your comfort zone
- Treat yourself with respect
- Have positive self-talk or affirmation sessions
- Track your progress
- Pursue passions that make you happy
- Allow yourself to be curious
- Dress for success
- Think about your big goals
- Stand up for yourself
- Read books, follow people on social media, or listen to podcasts that encourage self-confidence and positive self-talk

Building your confidence takes time and involves plenty of trials. As you put in the work toward being confident, here are a few tips to keep in mind:

- **Be proud of yourself:** Hard work deserves to be recognized. Maybe one of the ways that you're becoming more confident is by making more eye contact with people. You should also celebrate your smallest victories however you'd like. As you track your progress, make sure to think back to where you started. Think about how that version of you would be proud of where you are today.

- **Don't be afraid to open up:** It's often scary to be vulnerable to new people within your surroundings. But as you're learning new things and stepping outside of your comfort zone, don't be afraid to let yourself open up. Be present with where you are and what you're doing. As you grow, you can acknowledge your fears and worries, but don't let that prevent you from exposing yourself to new things.
- **Be specific:** Where do you lack confidence? Where are you super confident? Identifying these aspects will help you be specific with your goals. Discover what would give you confidence and start making purposeful actions toward obtaining it.
- **Go forth with confidence:** Even though self-confidence comes from within, reach out to friends and family for words of affirmation and encouragement to boost your self-esteem.
- **When walking alone, walk with purpose and project confidence:** Chin up, eyes forward, steady pace.
- **Always strive to feel, think, and speak positively about yourself:** Positive thoughts and words truly make a difference.

# Don't Let Your Past Define Your Future!

Some people have had trauma in their past. Several therapists shared their very personal stories with us and how they had to realize their past does not determine their future.

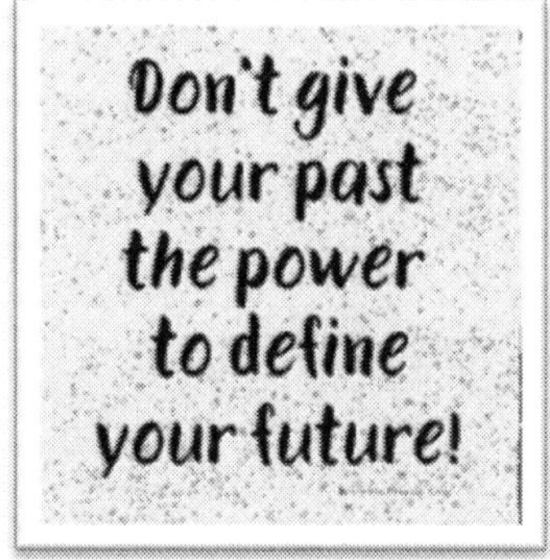


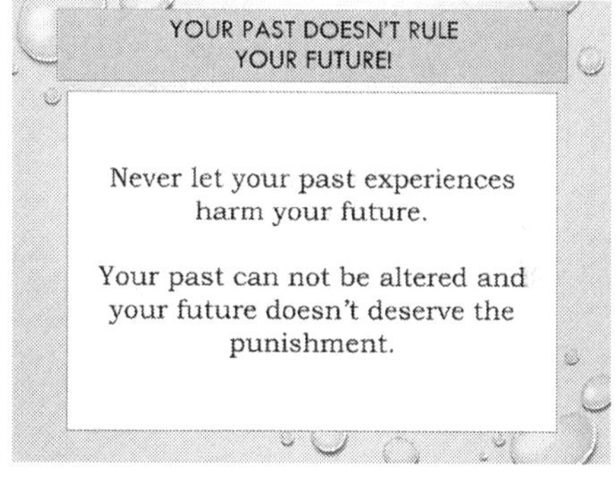


*We want you to be more confident by focusing on your potential, not on your limitations*

If you are the survivor of an assault, know that there are so many resources available, both local to you and online, to help you deal with residual fear, depression, or panic attacks. Never be afraid to be honest about the lasting effect your event has had and reach out.

We are all capable of greatness, so don't let your life situations or personal struggles pull you down. By knowing your personal gifts and talents and letting other people's strengths prevail where you are weak, both you and others will excel instead of being brought down by someone who is a bully. Challenge yourself to improve your weaknesses rather than dwell on them, and see your weaknesses as minor issues in your life, not failures.

Building confidence is a gradual process that involves self-awareness, practice, and positive reinforcement:

- **Challenge negative self-talk:** Practice positive self-talk. Pay attention to your inner dialogue. Replace negative thoughts with positive affirmations. For example, instead of thinking, "I can't do this," try, "I can learn how to do this."
- **Acquire new skills:** Engage in activities that interest you and allow you to develop new skills. This could be anything from learning a musical instrument, taking a cooking class, to learning martial arts.
- **Practice self-care:** Take care of your physical health through exercise, proper nutrition, and sufficient sleep. Feeling good physically can boost your mental state.
- **Surround yourself with positive people:** Spend time with supportive friends and family who encourage and uplift you. Their positivity can help reinforce your confidence.
- **Reflect on past successes:** Keep a journal of your accomplishments, big or small. Reminding yourself of past successes can help reinforce a positive self-image.
- **Embrace failure as a learning opportunity:** Understand that failure is part of growth. Instead of fearing it, view challenges as opportunities to learn and improve.

Building confidence takes time and effort, but with consistent practice and a positive mindset, you can cultivate a greater sense of self-assurance.

Rather than being judgmental or hostile toward other people's success, confident people celebrate others and feel genuine happiness for them rather than envy or comparison. Learning from others' successes inspires them. They don't rationalize others' successes or their own failures.

They may not be positive all the time, but they do keep a growth mindset. When they make a mistake, they usually can see the humor and are more likely to respond with laughter and easily overcome insecurity or shame.

People can be confident in specific areas of their lives, too. Some are more confident in their athletic abilities than their cooking expertise. Others might face a lack of confidence in certain academic subjects or dancing abilities.

In our class, we use the example of when we had to learn our multiplication tables in second grade. It was new to us. Once we learned how to multiply, we practiced over and over. I bet if I asked you, "What is eight times four?" you can tell me "thirty-two" with confidence! How did we know that with confidence?

We love baseball! Later in this book, we will look at a baseball player's quote in our self-care chapter. Here, we are using the example of a new player who's learning how to play. In teaching a five-year-old T-ball, they don't quite have the skills. They are learning body positions in order to hit and throw. Of course, they will continue to practice and gain confidence to stop a ball in the field or make contact with the bat. As they get older and go to the next level, they are hitting the pitched ball and making better throws and catches. The more coaching and practice the player has, the more it builds confidence and allows them to get better in their skill.

The areas where people feel self-confident often represent what they're most passionate about.

Using those examples, what do you see as a pattern? First, you need to learn the task. Then you need to practice over and over.

That's why you must always stay confident about your personal boundaries and practice building them up more!

**What would you do?**

*Adam, a male therapist and a former Army Ranger of considerable stature, had a male client on his table in a medical facility. The client, while prone, reached up and groped the therapist's inner thigh while moving his hand upward.*

*Find out what Adam did in Chapter 10.*

CHAPTER 4

# Situational Awareness

## How Aware Are You of Your Surroundings?

What if you are in a bank or store where someone just robbed the cashier? Could you give the police a positive ID of the person? What color shirt were they wearing? Did they have brown hair? How tall were they?

## Play the "WHAT IF?" Game

Look around right now. If there was a fire and you needed to escape the area, would you know where your closest and safest exit is? Do you see any items that can help you break a window if necessary?

Let's say you are at a grocery store or clothing store and someone needs medical attention. When you call 911, are you able to give the dispatcher the address of the store? Do you know a crossroad or landmark?

The same applies if you are driving down the highway and break down. Would you be able to give the mile marker or crossroad or landmark of where someone could find you?

If you find yourself in a bad situation and need to escape, are you thinking about where your exits are?

Understanding a threat assessment and levels of situational awareness is explained as follows.

A threat assessment is a process of observing, identifying, and reacting to a potential or immediate threat.

A crucial element in your personal safety is learning about the various levels of situational awareness and how those levels affect your capacity to react. These levels of awareness are most commonly referred to as "Cooper's Colors," and they serve as the basis for the system of awareness. These five levels give us an overview of situational awareness and the psychological states associated with each level.

What color of the spectrum do you live in? Have you driven home on "auto-pilot" and can't remember what you saw along the way? That would be in the Condition White. Or have you ever been on the opposite end of the spectrum where you may have panicked in a situation under extreme stress? That would be in the Condition Black.

Ideally, we want to be in Condition Yellow or even Condition Orange. Be aware of your surroundings and be able to identify a potential threat.

This chart is a Color Awareness Chart with color conditions.

| Condition White | Condition Yellow | Condition Orange | Condition Red | Condition Black |
|---|---|---|---|---|
| Unaware of your surroundings | General awareness | Recognize that a threat exists | Alarmed to an actual threat | Fight or flight Panic Mode-Stressed |
| Example: Driving home from a long day at work (on autopilot). Then, once home, does not remember the drive. | Example: While at work, you are in a state of relaxed awareness and notice what is going on around you. | Example: You observe a suspicious person walking around your neighbor's yard and you begin tactical planning. | Example: You initiate the plan to engage the suspects as they are in your sight. | Example: You are in panic mode and may not respond effectively. |

When it comes to maintaining proper situational awareness, condition yellow is where you want to be. You want to be in that casual yet observant state that allows you to take in as much information as possible without completely stressing yourself out.

## A Guide to Color Awareness Chart

The Color Awareness Chart is a framework used to evaluate and categorize threats based on their likelihood and potential impact.

- **White:** This level of situational awareness is most people's default setting. You are usually on code white at home, minding your business with locked doors.
- **Yellow:** This is the next immediate level. You hear neighbors in their yards.
- **Orange:** At this level, your head is on a swivel. The neighbors are having lots of visitors.
- **Red:** It is a code red! The neighbors are very loud and breaking bottles in the street.
- **Black:** TOO LATE!

| | |
|---|---|
| White | Unprepared and unready to take action. |
| Yellow | Prepared, alert & relaxed. Good situational awareness. |
| Orange | Alert to probable danger. Ready to take action. |
| Red | Action Mode. Focused on the emergency at hand. |
| Black | Panic. Breakdown of physical & mental performance. |

Here are some examples that illustrate different levels of threat along the spectrum:

**1. Low threat**

- **Personal boundary:** Minor phishing attempts to learn things about your private life.
- **Touch:** Accidental touch of the client's hand to the therapist's leg, where no harm was done.

**2. Moderate threat**

- **Personal boundary:** The client asks you out on a date to go for drinks.
- **Touch:** The client gently, but firmly holds the hand or arm of the therapist to establish control.

**3. High threat**

- **Personal boundary:** The client stands between the therapist and the exit, blocking the door.
- **Touch:** The client is violent toward the therapist.

**4. Severe threat**

- **Personal boundary:** The client grabs and picks up the therapist.
- **Touch:** This puts the therapist in a fight that might be the fight of your life.

**5. Catastrophic threat**

- **Personal boundary:** The client forces the therapist into a submissive position and gets on top of the therapist.
- **Touch:** This is now an attempted rape with lifelong implications for the therapist.

## Nothing Is as It Seems

Do you remember the movie “Pretty Woman?” Julia Roberts did not look like she was wealthy as she walked into the clothing store on Rodeo Drive. The employees did not want to give her any attention because they “assumed” she couldn’t afford their clothes based on her appearance. They did not know she had a credit card with no limit!

An acquaintance of mine is married to a good-looking, professional man who appears to be a good guy. What we do not see is when he gets home, he has an anger issue and beats his wife.

There are plenty of fascinating examples of people who are not what they seem, both in history and fiction. Here are a few more:

- **Hannibal Lecter** (from *The Silence of the Lambs*)**:** On the surface, he presents as a well-educated and sophisticated psychiatrist, but beneath that veneer lies a brilliant but psychopathic serial killer.
- **Walter White** (from *Breaking Bad*)**:** A high school chemistry teacher who transforms into a ruthless drug lord, his dual life reveals the darker side of a seemingly ordinary man.
- **Frank Abagnale** (*an imposter*)**:** Known for his life as a con artist, he impersonated various professionals, including a pilot and a doctor, all while being a teenager. His charm and intelligence masked his illegal activities.
- **Madoff Ponzi Scheme** (from *The Wizard of Lies*)**:** Bernie Madoff appeared to be a successful and trustworthy financier, but he was orchestrating one of the largest Ponzi schemes in history, deceiving countless investors.

Do you know anyone that LOOKS like they are the nicest, kindest, sincerest person? Do we really know what they are capable of?

What we see on the outside is not always the true perception. We must be on our toes and be aware that there could be more to a person than we see.

This "*apple*" has an appearance to be whole in the "*mirror*," but not so when we see it from a different angle; "*meaning*," we love to see only the good part and may not realize the entire picture.

Here is a favorite of mine that reminds us that nothing is as it seems:

## The Cookie Thief
### by Valerie Cox

A woman was waiting at an airport one night,
With several long hours before her flight.
She hunted for a book in the airport shops.
Bought a bag of cookies and found a place to drop.

She was engrossed in her book but happened to see,
That the man sitting beside her, as bold as could be.
Grabbed a cookie or two from the bag in between,
Which she tried to ignore to avoid a scene.

So she munched the cookies and watched the clock,
As the gutsy cookie thief diminished her stock.
She was getting more irritated as the minutes ticked by,
Thinking, "If I wasn't so nice, I would blacken his eye."

With each cookie she took, he took one too,
When only one was left, she wondered what he would do.
With a smile on his face, and a nervous laugh,
He took the last cookie and broke it in half.

He offered her half, as he ate the other,
She snatched it from him and thought... oooh, brother.
This guy has some nerve and he's also rude,
Why he didn't even show any gratitude!

She had never known when she had been so galled,
And sighed with relief when her flight was called.
She gathered her belongings and headed to the gate,
Refusing to look back at the thieving ingrate.

She boarded the plane, and sank in her seat,
Then she sought her book, which was almost complete.
As she reached in her baggage, she gasped with surprise,
There was her bag of cookies, in front of her eyes.

If mine are here, she moaned in despair,
The others were his, and he tried to share.
Too late to apologize, she realized with grief,
That she was the rude one, the ingrate, the thief.

This cute poem makes us realize that what we perceive is not always what is true.

## Perception

Can you look at a beautiful, petite woman and know for certain that she is as nice on the inside as on the outside? What's the chance that you look at her and know for certain that she is not carrying a weapon or has extensive martial arts training? Or can you look at her and know for certain that she will not steal from you?

Often, we want to believe people will do the right thing and will not bring harm to anyone, but we must be aware of our surroundings and stay on our toes.

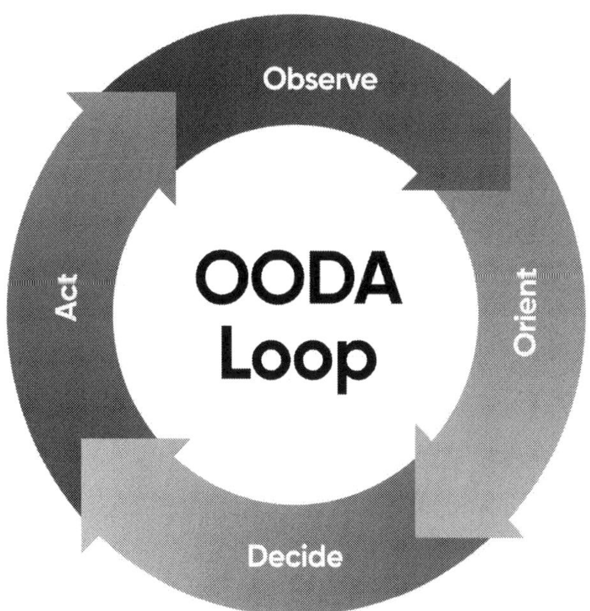


The above diagram "OODA Loop" is how we begin with an observation, which leads to orienting on options, then deciding on an appropriate course of action, and finally acting on that decision.

My son, Johnny, always tells my grandkids, "Keep your head on a swivel, especially when crossing the street or in the parking lot." This is the early teaching of situational awareness.

Why is situational awareness important? Do you remember when you were learning how to drive? We're always taught to look in all the mirrors before changing lanes. That is how we prepare ourselves to avoid getting hit by another car. That could also prevent our physical body from getting hurt, not just our car. The goal with situational awareness is not to let it consume you, or to be paranoid, but a way to use your eyes, ears, nose, and touch to observe and, with practice, it will come naturally.

## Situation Awareness Tips

Situational awareness involves being actively aware of your surroundings and potential threats or opportunities. Here are some key ways to improve your situational awareness:

- **Stay alert and observant:** Consciously pay attention to your environment, including people, objects, and potential exit routes.
- **Avoid distractions:** Limit the use of headphones or looking at your phone in public places.
- **Trust your instincts:** If something feels off, take it seriously and act accordingly.
- **Practice active listening:** Pay attention to conversations and sounds around you.
- **Scan your environment:** Regularly look around and assess your surroundings, especially when entering new areas.

- **Identify baseline behaviors:** Learn what's normal for an environment so you can spot anomalies.
- **Use peripheral vision:** Train yourself to notice things outside your immediate focus.
- **Stay informed:** Keep up with local news and events that might affect your safety.
- **Play the "what-if" game (plan ahead):** Think through potential scenarios and how you might respond.

Identifying potential threats from individuals requires careful observation and assessment. Some key indicators to watch for start with reading body language.

## Body Language

What do we want to look for when we observe someone's body language?

- **Scan the whole body:** Is there an immediate cause for concern?
- **Hands:** Are their hands visible? Are they holding anything?
- **Waistline:** Is there anything bulky or unusual?
- **Immediate area:** Is there a weapon within reach?
- **Demeanor:** Are they calm, a little jumpy, or have shifty eyes?

**1. Body language:**

- Aggressive posturing, fighting stance, or clenched fists
- Avoiding eye contact or staring intensely
- Invading personal space

**2. Behavioral cues:**

- Sudden mood changes or erratic behavior
- Appearing overly nervous or agitated
- Concealing hands or reaching for pockets/waistband

**3. Contextual factors:**

- Being in a high-crime area or isolated location
- Person seems out of place in the environment
- Group dynamics that suggest potential confrontation

**4. Verbal indicators:**

- Hostile or threatening language
- Slurred speech suggesting intoxication
- Rapid or pressured speech showing agitation

**5. Physical signs:**

- Visible weapons or bulges, suggesting concealed weapons
- Signs of intoxication or drug use
- Blood-shot eyes
- Sweating when they shouldn't be
- Unusual clothing choices (e.g., heavy coats in warm weather)

**6. Gut instinct:**

- Trust your intuition if something feels off

It's important to note that these indicators aren't definitive proof of a threat; rather, they're potential warning signs. Context is crucial, and it's best to err on the side of caution if you feel unsafe.

You never know when someone is carrying a concealed weapon or has extensive martial arts training.

**What would you do?**

*Julie, an experienced female colleague, accepted an out-call appointment with a male client. As she was setting up her table in the living room of the home, the client approached her from behind, wrapped his arms around her in a bear hug, lifted her up off of her feet, and carried her into the bedroom.*

*Find out what Julie did in Chapter 10.*

CHAPTER 5

# Treatment Room Safety

Bodyworkers offer their services in a wide variety of settings. Some massage therapists operate their own establishments, with some doing exclusively out-calls, some work as employees and others as independent contractors. The next chapter will deal more with the outcalls. This chapter will focus on the establishment setting.

Regardless of the environment, our collective intention is to provide a safe, comfortable, and therapeutic venue for ourselves and our clients.

Unfortunately, safety in our workspace often gets taken for granted, and it can be unnecessarily dangerous. If you haven't already, it's time to take ownership of your personal safety.

Now, therapists, it is time to show you how.

Let's begin by getting in touch with your tingly "spider-sense," just like Spiderman on TV has shown us to do.

Have you ever:

- Felt uneasy when a client's behavior crosses professional boundaries, unsure of how to respond?
- Felt vulnerable during late-night appointments, wishing you had the confidence and techniques to ensure your safety?
- Had a sense of concern when a client became unexpectedly agitated, leaving you uncertain how to de-escalate the situation without compromising your safety?

Now that we have awakened one or more of those memories, pick one and see what message they have for you in your current work environment—not for being fearful as much as being awake and cautious.

Several male and female therapists have encountered situations in different clinical massage environments that have made them feel uneasy or, perhaps, even threatened. Over the decades, our friends and colleagues have shared their stories with us, which prompted us to share how we can help other practitioners feel safer in their day-to-day operations.

As an owner of a massage school for almost three decades, our students get trained to become high-performing professionals in the commercial healthcare setting. In addition to the required curriculum, instruction on proper communication is critical, both verbal and non-verbal. It includes the initial contact, entrance into the treatment room, and how to end the session. Professional communication begins with the proper attitude, as professional body language portrays being a confident therapist, knowing how to maintain your safety in and out of the treatment room.

We have complete control over what we offer, but limited control of its perception. We know what we wish to do, but do not know what the client wishes to do.

Let's think about control. What do you have control of? If you are interested in nutritional health, you have control over what you take in, caloric intake, and nutritional value. When we are working on a client, how do we take control? Why wouldn't we want to control how we can stay safe in our clinic, establishment, hospital, office, or any other healthcare setting? Once you know how, you can easily practice protocols and prevent being vulnerable by being aware and staying safe.

**"An ounce of prevention is worth a pound of cure."**
**Benjamin Franklin**

## Setting the Stage

The first step in protecting yourself as a massage therapist isn't necessarily taking a self-defense class, although that's a wise choice for anyone in today's world. The first safety step for massage professionals is properly setting up the stage—it's the old "ounce of prevention" notion. You can avoid most of the unpleasant situations entirely by planning wisely.

For example, when choosing a location for your office, be smart. Choose a well-lit area where there will commonly be plenty of traffic during the hours you will operate. Don't be the only place open, the only car in the lot. Set up your practice so that you don't look like a target. Examine nearby businesses and think about the sort of impression a walk-in client might get. Use the same criteria if you are considering employment in an existing spa or clinic.

Another way to set the stage is to evaluate your advertising to ensure you convey a professional tone. Your business cards should include your full credentials so that potential clients understand the service you provide is therapeutic and professional.

Give some thought to your basic setup. Place the massage table and other furnishings so that you will naturally tend to keep yourself between the client and the door as much as possible throughout the session. You should never need to turn your back on a client who is not on the table.

In order for you to do your very best work, you need to feel completely safe and secure in your therapeutic room. This is your sacred place where you can and should be the most in control.

Right from the beginning, you must take control. The first point of contact: there needs to be proper communication portraying verbal confidence. This can be via phone, text, or email. When they come in, always be professional with your words and communicate physical confidence. You control how you look at them, how you introduce yourself, how you communicate, and how you physically work on them in the treatment room. Professional attire will also send an appropriate signal. Don't set yourself up to be misunderstood. Resist the temptation to dress informally and keep jewelry to a minimum.

In the initial in-person greeting, look the client in the eyes, reach out, and present a firm handshake. Once you take them into the treatment room and instruct them to get undressed to their level of comfort and under the sheet, you may also assure them they will be completely draped at all times. Always use proper draping! Always make sure a female's chest is covered. This can be done with the flat sheet and blanket, or by adding a towel to protect the client's modesty. Use draping over the glutes on both male and female clients. Using a sheet or towel over the glutes serves a couple of different purposes. The client feels safe and comfortable and it protects you from being accused of touching them inappropriately. It also provides a barrier and gives you the ability to work the area without slipping, which can happen if you are skin-to-skin.

In the previous chapter, we described situational awareness tips. Awareness allows us to be prepared and avoid a potentially dangerous situation. Avoiding that danger is the best-case scenario in any (healthcare) setting. By staying alert and carefully planning, you can enhance your safety while doing what you love!

## Proper Procedures Lead to Peace of Mind

Thinking about personal safety is often the furthest thing from your mind as you work to provide professional services in a serene environment. In fact, a practitioner's nurturing mindset can cause resistance to taking even the simplest of cautionary steps.

Healthcare professionals are very caring individuals. Choosing this profession means you want to help others to heal and be well. The thought that someone wants to do harm to another isn't usually on the radar of a healthcare professional. But what if they do? What would you do? You must remember to always set personal boundaries to protect yourself from inappropriate and unacceptable behavior.

## Personal Boundaries

Boundaries serve as guidelines that help to maintain a healthy level of separation between different aspects of our lives. By defining personal and professional boundaries, we define expectations, set limits, and establish respectful relationships with ourselves and others.

Developing professional personal boundaries means clearly defining the limits of your professional interactions, separating your personal life from your work life, and communicating these boundaries effectively to clients, or anyone you interact with professionally, ensuring a healthy work environment and preventing potential conflicts or overstepping of personal space.

Personal boundaries are sets of guidelines that determine how we interact with others, how we take care of ourselves, and how we allow others to treat us. These boundaries are essential for maintaining emotional, physical, and mental well-being.

What are some ways to take control of an uncomfortable situation? You have the control in the treatment room. We can practice protocols and prevent being vulnerable by being aware and staying safe.

A first-year female therapist shared with me how she followed her gut and maintained personal boundaries. Her male client, who was very wealthy, had seen her several times. "He was polite, but weird," she shared with me. He asked her personal questions that made her feel uneasy. Immediately, she said, "This session is for you. My personal life is irrelevant." Her response made him a bit aggravated, and he said he was just wanting to get to know her. She continued to be strong in her verbal communication. Even though she really needed the income, she fired him as a client. Her explanation was that she had "Zero Tolerance" for inappropriate language or behavior.

Key aspects of developing professional personal boundaries:

- **Know your limits:** Understand what you are comfortable sharing and doing within a professional setting, including sharing personal information.
- **Communicate clearly:** Directly express your boundaries to others, using assertive language and setting clear expectations about what is professional behavior.
- **Set working hours:** Establish clear start and end times for your workday and respect them.
- **Avoid dual relationships:** Be cautious about engaging in personal relationships with clients that could create conflicts of interest.
- **Physical boundaries:** Respect personal space and physical contact, avoid inappropriate gestures or behaviors.

- **Digital boundaries:** Manage professional communication channels like email and social media appropriately.
- **Say no when necessary:** Be comfortable in declining requests that fall outside your scope of work or could compromise your boundaries.
- **Be mindful of appearance:** Dress and present yourself professionally in accordance with your workplace expectations.
- **Seek guidance if needed:** If you are unsure about setting boundaries in a specific situation, consult with a supervisor or mentor.

Some examples of professional boundaries in the workplace:

- Not discussing personal issues with clients.
- Maintaining an appropriate professional demeanor during any interaction.
- Setting limits on after-hours communication.

Here are some reasons why professional boundaries are important:

- **Builds trust:** Clear boundaries foster a sense of professionalism and respect within the workplace.
- **Maintains ethical conduct:** Setting limits helps to avoid potential conflicts of interest or inappropriate behavior.

- **Improves work-life balance:** Separating personal and professional life allows for better mental health and well-being.

## Clear Communication

Imagine a situation where a client constantly probes and/or crosses your emotional boundaries by making insensitive remarks. By establishing and communicating clear personal boundaries, you can express how their words make you feel and establish a healthier and more respectful relationship.

Creating boundaries is a personal journey that requires self-awareness, reflection, and assertiveness. Some practical ways to do this include:

- **Communicate your boundaries:** Clearly articulate, verbally and nonverbally, your boundaries to others. For instance, if you have a tendency to receive calls during your personal time, you can express to your clients the importance of preserving that time for personal commitments.
- **Learn to say no:** Setting limits by saying no when necessary is an essential part of boundary-setting. For example, if you already have a heavy workload and the client wishes to book with you, it is important to assess your capacity to set limitations appropriately.

Set boundaries to provide structure and create the necessary space for your personal growth and success. Rather than restricting you, it does quite the opposite by allowing you to lead a healthier and happier life that fulfills you.

While we only wish to think the best of our clients, there are instances, many unreported, when that has not truly been the case. The challenge may be physical, emotional, or likely, both. It seems clear—the need to protect ourselves must be part of our initial and ongoing professional education. In any difficult situation, being able to respond confidently is the intended outcome.

How can we give a client a sense of security and let them know you are in control, but at the same time, give the best treatment? It starts with our intent.

My teachings include starting the client supine. This gives you a way to not only assess anterior visual imbalances but also gives you the opportunity to see their face while you are working on them. Your touch should be one that makes them feel secure and safe.

One example: when you are working on a client's arm, hold the wrist and give a slight traction while keeping the arm on the table. It gives you an elongated arm, allowing your stroke to be efficient. The client will feel secure and feel that you are in control.

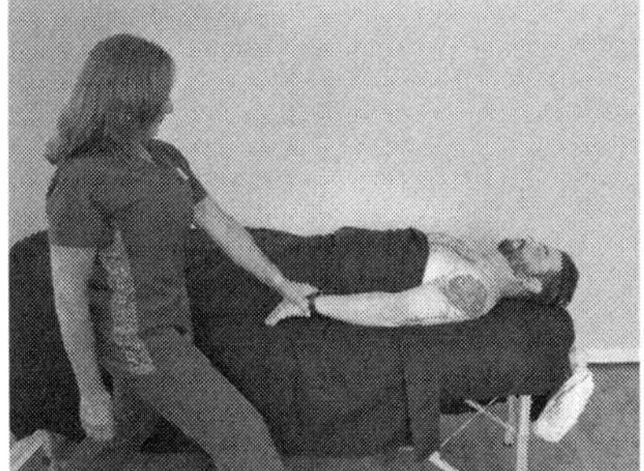

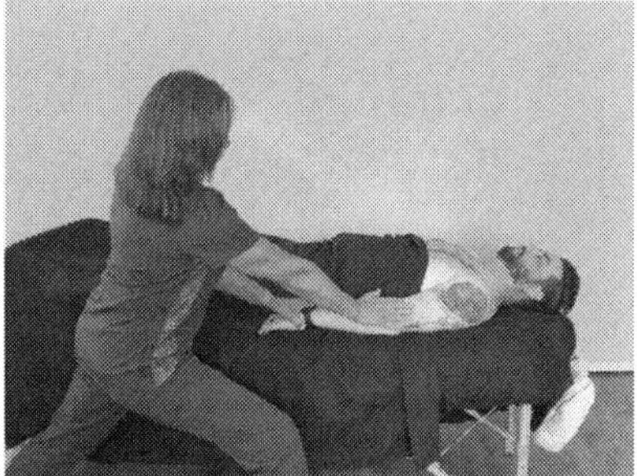

With male or female clients, Range of Motion (ROM) and stretching techniques are techniques where draping skills are necessary. Using secure draping on the legs will provide security for both you and the client. Take the drape under the leg to be stretched, pull it up to the hip, then ask the client to hold the two ends of the sheet in order for the stretching to be performed and nothing gets exposed.

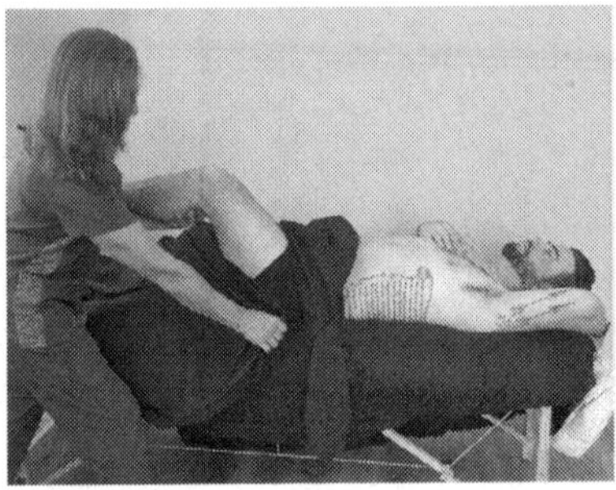

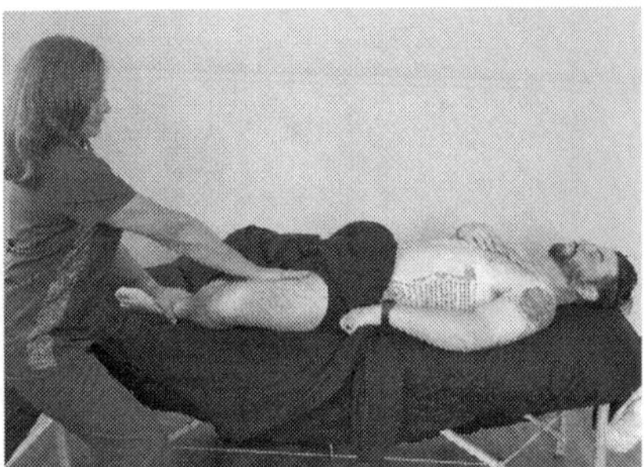

When working on a male client and you're using a sheet, this draping is totally secure. If there is a legit upper adductor (groin) issue on a male client that needs work, confidently work in this area. You can use the same draping for a female client. Proper draping will let the client be aware of your professionalism.

Other than your hands, forearms, or feet that you are using to apply your strokes, no other body part should touch the client. It could happen by accident, so be cautious. You must also be very mindful not to have your breasts, stomach, thigh, or anything (even your loose shirt) touch the client.

We talked about confidence in a previous chapter. Practicing communication and physical confidence will come naturally in time. You should also follow de-escalation strategies, which can be both verbal and physical.

**De-escalation tactics** are strategies used to calm a tense situation or resolve conflict and include active listening, being empathetic, and using nonthreatening language. These strategies also count maintaining a calm demeanor, actively listening to the other person, validating their emotions, using non-judgmental language, respecting personal space, offering choices when possible, avoiding confrontational body language, and focusing on understanding the underlying issues rather than reacting to immediate anger or frustration.

Key elements of verbal de-escalation:

- **Be calm:** Remain calm and regulated.
- **Active listening:** Pay full attention to what the person is saying, using verbal and non-verbal cues to show you are engaged.
- **Empathy:** Try to understand the other person's perspective and emotions, acknowledging their feelings without dismissing them.
- **Non-threatening language:** Use simple, clear language and avoid accusatory or provocative phrases.
- **Be nonjudgmental:** Avoid judging the other person.
- **Seeking assistance:** If needed, involve a third party who can help mediate the situation.
- **Maintaining composure:** Stay calm and avoid mirroring the other person's anger or aggression.
- **Respecting personal space:** Give the other person room and avoid physically crowding them.
- **Validating concerns:** Acknowledge the legitimacy of their issues and concerns.

- **Offering choices:** Where appropriate, give the other person options to feel more in control.

What to avoid when de-escalating:

- **Arguing or debating:** Don't try to prove the other person wrong or engage in a power struggle.
- **Making assumptions:** Avoid jumping to conclusions about the situation or the other person's motives.
- **Using threats or ultimatums:** This can escalate the situation further.
- **Ignoring the person's concerns:** Dismissively brushing off their feelings can make them feel unheard and more frustrated.

## Verbal Communication

First of all, trust yourself! If you feel like something is off, it probably is. Don't wait to address the issue because you are trying to figure out if something is just in your head. It is real!

If you have a client making inappropriate comments, reply with:

"I am a trained and licensed massage therapist. I offer therapeutic work only."

"I am not going to continue this session if you speak to me in that manner."

"I do not appreciate that. If you want me to continue, your inappropriate comments must stop."

"You signed the intake form that you understood our policies. I will collect your full payment. I take situations like this very seriously!"

I'm sorry to say that handling things like this is a reality in our massage world and in other professions. Arm yourself with these tools so that when that day comes, you will know how to react in an effective, prepared manner! Trust yourself and speak with confidence and power.

So what about when you have taken all the precautions and you still have inappropriate requests?

If you feel your safety is in jeopardy, leave the treatment room and call 911.

NEVER compromise your safety. Remember, "NO" means no! No one has the right to violate your space or decision. Stand up for yourself and don't back down. Terminate the session immediately if necessary!

## Safety Tips for Your Establishment/Clinic/ Hospital/Building

- Have a "Security System" sign. (Even if you do not have a security system.)
- Have cameras in the foyer.
- Keep weapons in different rooms—baseball bat by the door, knives, guns, hammers, or even spray cleaners. (Get familiar with how to handle them.)
- Check your surroundings before you get out of your car to go into your establishment.

- Have a deadbolt or more than one lock on your door if you are there alone or after hours. NEVER let your client know you are alone.
- **Install security systems:** Use a reliable alarm system and security cameras.
- **Use outdoor lighting:** Install effective outdoor lighting, such as yard lighting, to deter criminals. You can also use light timers to turn your lights on and off at specific times.
- **Trim shrubs and trees:** Burglars like to hide behind shrubs while they pry open windows, so keep shrubs trimmed.
- **Use a secure safe:** Keep cash in a secure safe. A hidden floor safe is a great choice.

**What would you do?**

*Jessica was called to a renowned hotel to a professional soccer player's room. She was setting up her table while the soccer player was in the restroom. Jessica looks up as he comes out of the restroom to see him standing there totally naked.*

*Find out what Jessica did in Chapter 10.*

CHAPTER 6

# Outcall Safety

Many massage therapists offer outcalls for their clients. It may entail going to someone's home, office, or hotel. To ensure safety during a massage outcall, a therapist should follow certain procedures and have their own protocol. Everything mentioned in the previous chapter does not change. The difference with an outcall is you are now in their territory. This may give the client an advantage. We still need to remember that "an ounce of prevention is worth a pound of cure."

## Are We Setting the Stage for Outcall Safety?

Start with your advertising.

- Does it have a professional look?
- Are you listing all your credentials and appropriate license numbers?
- Do you have your specific modalities/specialties listed?
- Are you advertising your website?

- Do you have a code of conduct statement?
- Do you verbalize your ethical, professional, nonsensual, and nonsexual services? You could state "Inappropriate requests are not tolerated" and mention draping is a requirement.

An outcall appointment may start with a phone call or email. We should ask them questions that will give us a secure feeling that they want a professional therapeutic massage. What questions do we want to ask the potential client? Our questions need to be professional and open-ended. Tailor your questions so they will give insight into what you need to know. This will give them the opportunity to share information with you that will be specific and allow you to create a signature massage and at the same time, rule out any unwelcomed client.

During the initial call, we need to ask professional questions that will determine if our therapeutic massage fits their needs. Our questions will lead to answers that will give us peace of mind that the potential client and their location will allow us to stay safe. It can also help raise a red flag, which can identify a potential problem. So, be alert during the verbal intake.

Red flags are those little alarms that go off in your head, warning you that this appointment or client isn't right for you or isn't looking for professional massage therapy services—they are looking for something else. Safety is critical, and if something doesn't feel right, don't book the appointment.

In speaking to them, we need to ask:

- **May I have your full name?**
    - Research to find them on any social media or their business page.

- **May I have your phone number?**
  - There may be access to do a reverse lookup by using their phone number.
- **How did you hear about me? Or how did you get my name?**
  - If they tell you a site that you do not advertise on, that is a red flag.
  - Is it from a referral? Verify from who and how they know that person.
  - Was it through an LMT locator?
- **What is the address of your home?**
  - Look up the address to see if it is within your travel radius.
  - Verify it is in an area you are comfortable traveling to.
  - Verify they are the homeowner.
- **If at a home:**
  - What room will I be able to set up my table?
  - Is there enough space?
  - Is this on the first floor or the second floor?
  - Is there ample parking?
  - Will anyone else be home at the time?
- **If at a hotel:**
  - Look up the address to see if it is within your travel radius.

- Verify it is in an area you are comfortable traveling to.
- Will anyone else be in the room with you?

- **Reason for the session:**
  - Do you have any specific problem area? Anything giving you an issue?
  - Is your pain/issue because of an activity?
  - How long has this been going on?
  - Is this issue affecting your job?
  - Do you have any recent injuries?
  - Is there anything about your health/physical condition you think I need to know about?
- **Day/Time:**
  - What day and time are you hoping to schedule an appointment?

For a massage therapist's own peace of mind, remember to keep these safety precautions to put in place:

- **Communication with someone you trust:**
  - Inform a trusted friend, family member, or partner about the client's name, address, and expected time of the massage.
  - Check-in with your contact before starting the massage and when leaving the appointment.
  - Consider using location-sharing apps to allow your safety contact to track your whereabouts.

- **Call a contact person:**
  - o Once in the room—and in front of the client—call somebody to let that person know you're starting the massage.
  - o Calling does two things. One—it lets the client know that someone knows where you are and, two—it lets your contact person know when you should call back. If you don't call back in the agreed-upon time frame, instruct the contact person to call the front desk. Let your client hear your phone call telling someone where you are and what time you will be home. Letting the client know that someone else knows where you are adds a layer of protection.
  - o When you finish with your massage session and in your car, you should call your contact person again and let them know you are safe, and share where you are heading next.
- **Location awareness:**
  - o If visiting a hotel, inform the front desk of your presence and the room number.
  - o Ask if there is an employee to help take your table to the client's room and in front of the client, ask the employee to come back at a certain time to help you carry your table back down.
- **Boundary setting:**
  - o Clearly communicate your professional boundaries and refuse any inappropriate requests.

    - Be prepared to end the session if a client crosses boundaries.
- **Physical safety measures:**
    - Carry a fully charged phone and have access to emergency numbers.
    - Consider carrying a personal alarm or whistle.
    - Ensure the massage room is well-lit and has easy access to an exit.
- **Trust your instincts:**
    - If something feels off about a client or situation, do not hesitate to cancel the appointment or leave immediately.
- **Professional appearance and demeanor:**
    - Dress professionally and maintain a confident posture to project a sense of authority.

Proper setup and strong, clear intake policies go a long way in protecting yourself from inappropriate behavior. With those safeguards, most clients will not be a cause for concern. However, you still need to recognize and stay prepared to deal with clients whose expectations or actions are unacceptable. Be ready to say no, to end the session, and leave.

Not all inappropriate requests lead to physical confrontations. Despite your stage setting and intake procedures, the client may have misunderstood the nature of your practice. The client still may simply get confused as to the boundaries of therapeutic massage contact. Firmly explain that you only provide professional therapeutic massage and that the request is inappropriate. It is possible, after making this clear and seeing that the client truly understands, that the session could continue if you are comfortable with the situation. If not, do not be reluctant to end the session and leave.

With these initial questions and safeguards, most clients will not be a cause for concern. You still need to recognize and be prepared to deal with clients whose expectations or actions are unacceptable. Once again, be ready to say no, to end the session if needed, and simply leave.

Intuition is a valuable safety net. Follow your gut. If it doesn't feel right, it probably isn't right. Don't be afraid to walk away from a massage. Your safety is worth it.

**Questions a client may ask that are not massage related:**

- Asking for your photo or sending a photo of themselves: You can simply ignore the message or respond that you work with referrals only.
- Asking about your relationship status: Keep your personal life private.
- Asking about draping: Always use proper draping. Explain to the client that you'll drape them for the entire massage. The sheet is adjusted to uncover only the areas of the body that are receiving therapeutic massage.
- Asking if you offer extra or special services.

These questions would raise a red flag and give you the right to refuse them as a client.

- **Unusual request:** For example, if a client asks for inner thigh work, it may be a red flag, but not always—for example, many athletes require upper thigh work. So, if someone legitimately needs work in these areas, they will usually specify why. They may say they got injured playing a sport, etcetera. Use the proper draping procedures described in the previous chapter.
- **If a new client is calling or texting after hours:** Do not answer the phone or reply to any messages after hours.
- **Trust your gut:** You have the right to refuse.

Are you working in condition yellow? What exactly aroused your suspicion and shifted you from condition yellow to condition orange? You feel comfortable in these surroundings and everything seems to be well within the baseline. You are maintaining a "condition-yellow" state of awareness.

After you give a verbal warning and all the precautions, if you still face inappropriate comments or behavior—then terminate the session.

Keep your phone in your pocket. Call 911 if you feel you are in danger or feel threatened. Leave your table and get to a safe location. You can always replace your equipment and table, but YOU CAN NEVER GET REPLACED!

**What would you do?**

*A 6'2" male therapist, Henry, shared they have been working on female client once a month for nine months. On the next visit, he was ending a two-hour, deep tissue session with a cranial hold. The female client reached up over her head and sensually caressed Henry's arms.*

*Find out what Henry did in Chapter 10.*

CHAPTER 7

# Introduction to Basic Self-Defense

## When Verbal Communication Is Not Enough

How do we physically defend ourselves from a client who presents inappropriate behavior?

Do you know how you would react or what you would do if a client touched you inappropriately? Having great verbal confidence, physical confidence, situational awareness, and knowing the safety tips to avoid a dangerous situation are ways to stay safe and deter inappropriate behavior. What would you do if the situation escalates and the client does not stand down?

This chapter will describe physical ways to handle and get out of a situation should it escalate. There are several things to keep in mind as we are fighting for our lives. There is no "one size fits all." This means that you will probably have to use multiple strikes or techniques before you can remove yourself from the situation.

We have verbally and confidently tried to de-escalate an uncomfortable situation, but our client has gotten a little more aggressive while they are on the table. In such cases, we can use pressure points on a client. The following pressure points are physical ways that can cause pain and let them know you are not putting up with their abuse.

Pressure points are areas on the body that can cause pain and/or discomfort. While the client is supine on the table, you can use the following pressure points in conjunction with you verbally telling them to halt their behavior. Pressure points are used to deter them from doing anything further to bring you harm and make the client know you will not tolerate any inappropriate behavior.

Here, we will show you four pressure points that are usually very effective while a client is supine on the table.

## PRESSURE POINTS

1. **Under the jaw**
   (mandible angle)
2. **Hollow behind the ear**
3. **Under the nose**
4. **Hollow of the neck**
   (sternoclavicular notch)

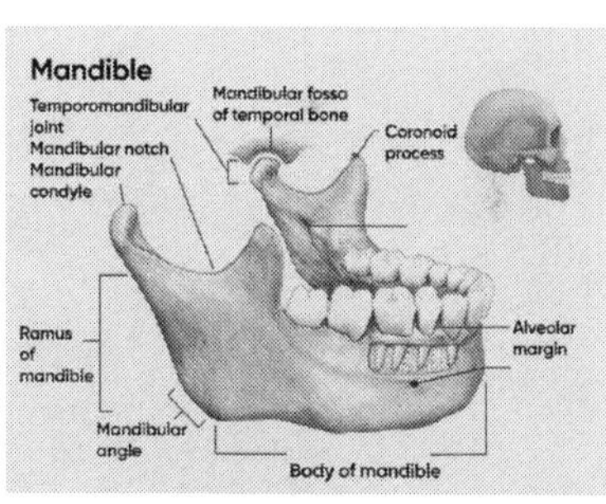


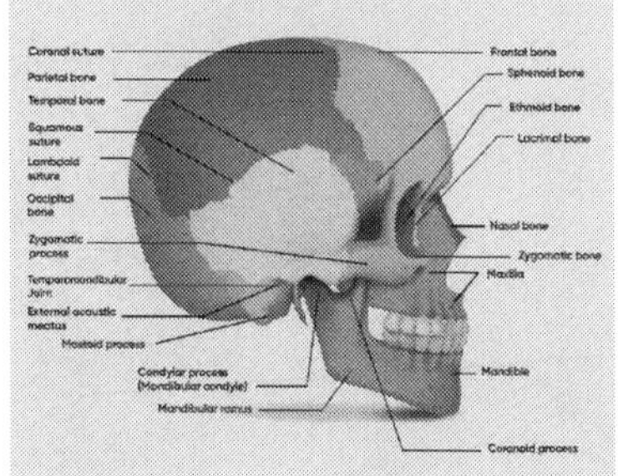

Hook fingers under the jaw. Push in while pulling up.

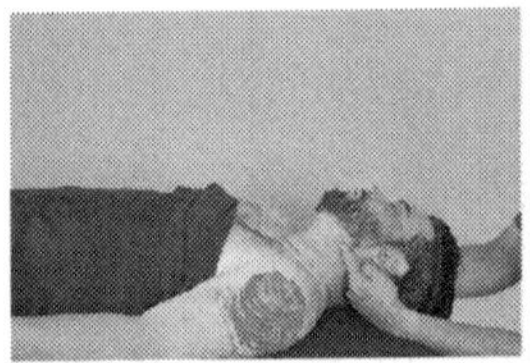
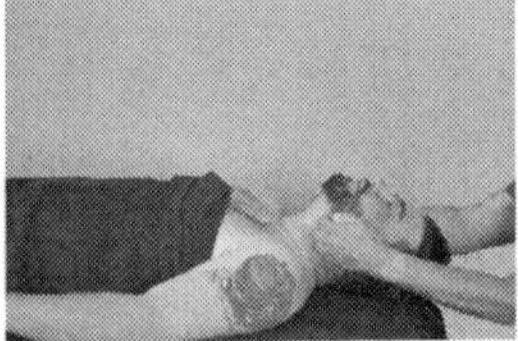
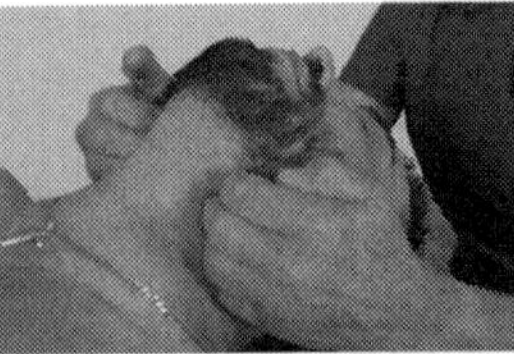

*Under the jaw*

Using your fingertips (I like to use my middle finger), press firmly in and up in the hollow of the ear.

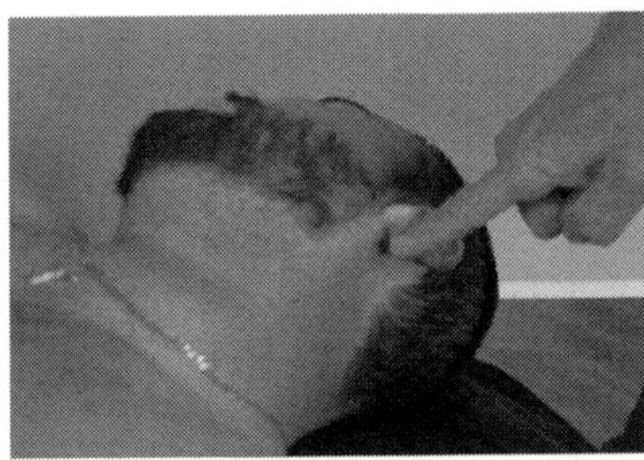
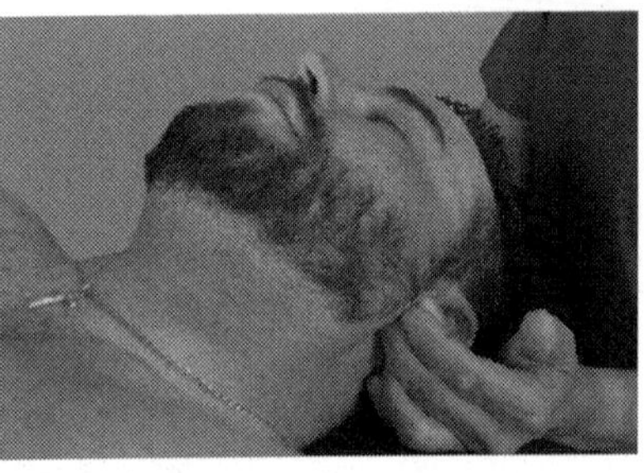

*Hollow behind the ear*

The nose is very sensitive on its own. Put pressure below the nose or at the base of the nose with a firm hand or a palm heel strike.

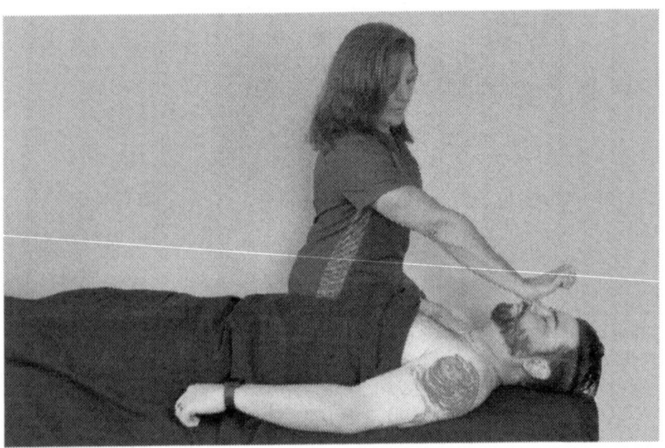

*Under the nose*

We call this the "Sit-down button." Using your firm fingertips, press in and down in the Sternal notch. It will make the person get pushed back down.

*Hollow of the neck*

**Base of the throat:** Feel that little notch between your clavicles? Press it with two fingers. Uncomfortable, yes? This is one of the most effective places to jab an attacker. With a firm, pointed hand, jab that notch at the base of the throat. Your attacker will be surprised and will be gasping or coughing uncontrollably. Use the moment break and run if possible. Their coughing will be throwing off their ability to hang on to you effectively.

We coined this move as the "sit-down button." If someone is getting up, put pressure at the base of the throat and they will get back down.

# Joint Manipulation

We, massage therapists, understand the body and how it moves. We know the action of a joint. Here, we will show you a few joint manipulations that can control a client while they are on the table. Joint manipulation techniques are often associated with martial arts, self-defense, law enforcement, or therapeutic practices, and you can use them to control a person in a nonlethal manner.

However, apply these techniques responsibly, ethically, and with proper training to ensure safety. Below are some common joint manipulation techniques that are typically used in various contexts:

**1. Arm bar (leveraging the elbow):**

- **Application:** This technique applies pressure to the elbow joint by hyper-extending it. The application is when the client's arm is isolated, and the practitioner uses their body weight to bend the arm backward to control the client.
- **Objective:** To create leverage and discomfort, which may force compliance or submission.

**2. Wrist lock:**

- **Application:** The wrist lock involves controlling the wrist joint by rotating it in an unnatural direction. It often gets used in law enforcement and self-defense to restrain someone without causing injury.
- **Objective:** The goal is to create pain and control through the wrist's range of motion. You can perform it

from various angles and positions, even if the person is in a standing or seated position.

**3. Shoulder lock:**

- **Application:** This technique targets the shoulder joint by isolating the arm and creating a lock that rotates the shoulder outward. It is commonly used in Brazilian jiu-jitsu and submission grappling.
- **Objective:** By forcing the arm into an unnatural position, the person is forced to submit or comply to avoid injury to the shoulder.

**4. Straight arm lock:**

- **Application:** This involves locking the arm straight and applying pressure to the elbow, causing pain and discomfort. One can use it in self-defense and law enforcement scenarios.
- **Objective:** This technique can force the individual to the ground or restrict their movement.

**5. Finger locks:**

- **Application:** Similar to wrist locks, finger locks manipulate the fingers, often targeting the thumb or middle fingers. The goal is to create pain and discomfort by bending the fingers unnaturally.
- **Objective:** This technique can cause pain and provide control by limiting the person's ability to fight back.

**6. Hammerlock:**

- **Application:** The hammerlock is a shoulder lock that involves manipulating the arm behind the back. The arm is bent in such a way that it forces the shoulder joint into an uncomfortable or painful position.

- **Objective:** To subdue or restrain someone without causing permanent damage to the joint.

**Important considerations:**

- **Safety:** Always apply joint manipulation techniques with caution. Improper application can cause permanent damage to joints, ligaments, or muscles.
- **Training:** Proper training in the techniques is essential for safety and effectiveness. Always learn these techniques under the supervision of qualified instructors.
- **Legal and ethical use:** Only use joint manipulation techniques when necessary, such as in self-defense or law enforcement situations. It's important to understand the legal implications of using force.

If you're interested in learning joint manipulation techniques for self-defense, it's best to enroll in a reputable class or program under a qualified instructor to ensure proper technique and safety.

## *Joint manipulation used on a client*

Push/roll triceps above the elbow toward the body, while controlling the hand/wrist turning the thumb down.

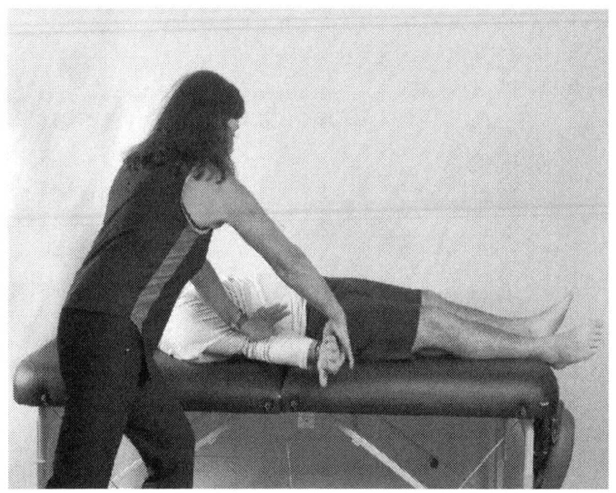

*With the client supine*

Control wrist/hand turning thumb down, while putting pressure on the triceps.

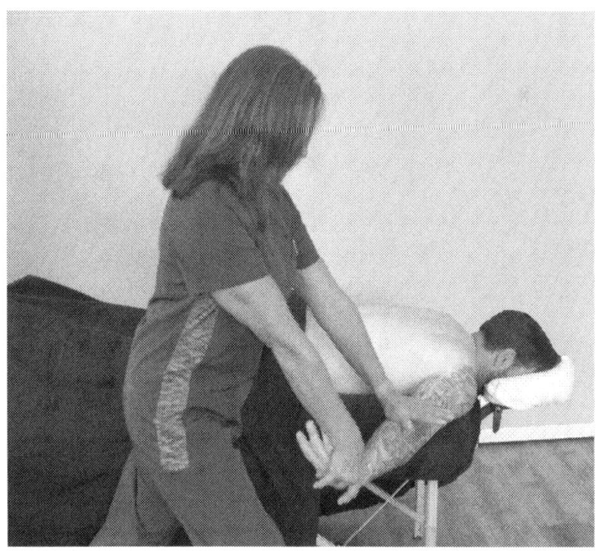

*With the client prone*

## *Physical Defense Tactics*

Recognizing the importance of physical defense tactics, healthcare workers must equip themselves with a variety of practical self-defense techniques to address immediate threats effectively. One essential technique is the "wrist grab escape." This maneuver is particularly useful if a person grabs your arm. To perform it, relax your arm momentarily, then make a fist with your thumb up. Then swiftly rotate your wrist toward the person's thumb and pull it free. This action exploits the natural weakness in the grip, allowing your arm to break loose.

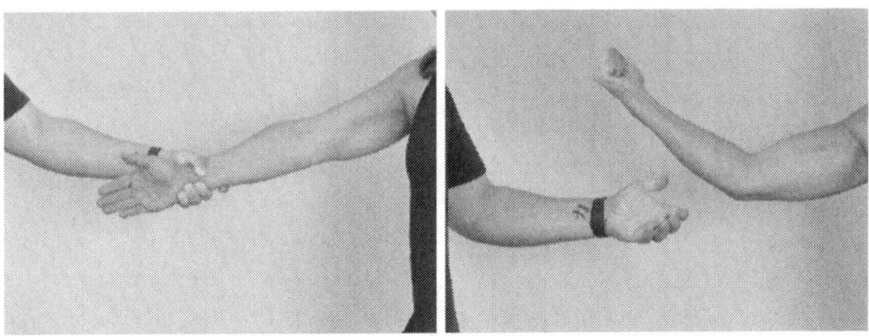

Another useful tactic is the "stomp-and-run" technique. If you find yourself in close quarters with an aggressor, aim a forceful stomp on their foot using your heel. This can cause significant pain and distraction, giving you a chance to escape quickly. Healthcare environments often have limited escape routes, so always be mindful of your surroundings and mentally map out paths to safety.

Further, the ability to employ a "basic strike" can create opportunities for you to evade a threat. A simple yet effective technique is the "palm heel strike." Curl your fingers and use the heel of your palm to drive upward into the attacker's chin or nose. This motion doesn't require much strength but can destabilize an aggressor, providing a critical moment to get away. Another effective technique is the "elbow strike," especially in close quarters where punches might be challenging to execute. Raise your elbow to shoulder height and drive it forcefully into the attacker's torso or head. Using your opposite hand to enforce the drive will give you more power.

This technique is powerful and can cause significant discomfort, allowing you to neutralize the threat. Moreover, using barriers available in your environment, such as chairs or carts, can also be advantageous. Placing such an object between you and the aggressor can provide a temporary shield and buy you essential time. Integrating these physical defense tactics into your skill set will not only prepare you for unforeseen challenges, but also enhance your overall security and peace of mind.

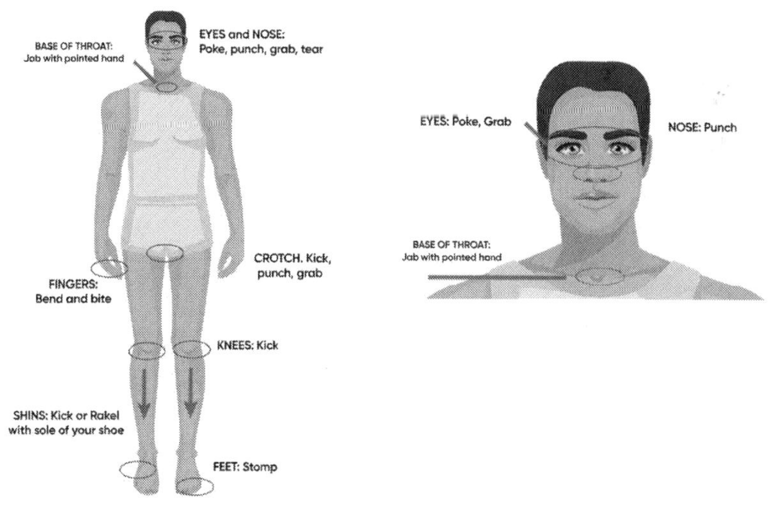


When we need to strike, there are sensitive target areas we can aim for.

**Target areas:**

- Eyes
- Ears
- Throat
- Nose
- Groin
- Knees

Keep these target areas in mind when you must become physical.

Your attacker has several weak spots that you can take quick advantage of. Use any or all of these if they grab you. Wherever you are causing discomfort, that's where your attacker's mind goes. You want to get his mind off of his grip on you. Drawing his focus to other places increases your chances of breaking his grip. The goal is to disrupt the attack so you can break free and RUN.

**Eyes:** Gnarl your fingers into a claw hand. Grab, tear, and poke at the attacker's eyes. They will want to get your hands away from their face and will have to loosen their grip or adjust their hold to do so. This is when you break and run.

**Nose**: A place where it really hurts to get hit. A forceful upward palm heel strike is extremely effective (as shown below during one of our classes). If your hands are restrained, use a headbutt to smash the nose.

**Fingers:** Bend them backward, bite them, stomp on them, etc.

**Groin:** A kick, a fist, or a knee to the groin area can definitely cause someone enough pain to let you get away.

**Foot stomp:** Stomp with everything you've got! Anything you can do to throw off your attacker's balance is in your favor. They're unlikely to do a good job of holding on to you if they're falling over. You're also drawing focus away from their grasp on you.

Drive your thumbs through the eyeballs!

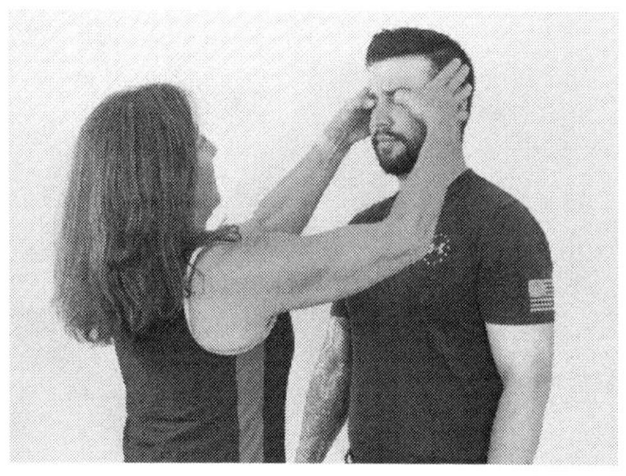

*Eyes*

With a palm heal strike, drive the heel of your hand up and through their head!

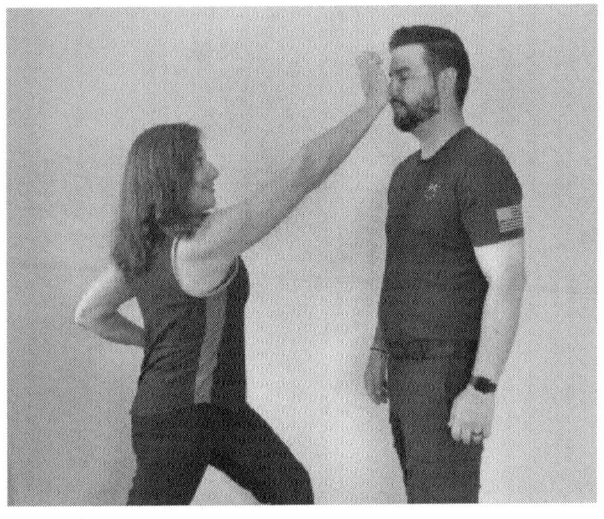

*Nose*

Box their ears with force! (Clap your hands hard with their head between your hands!)

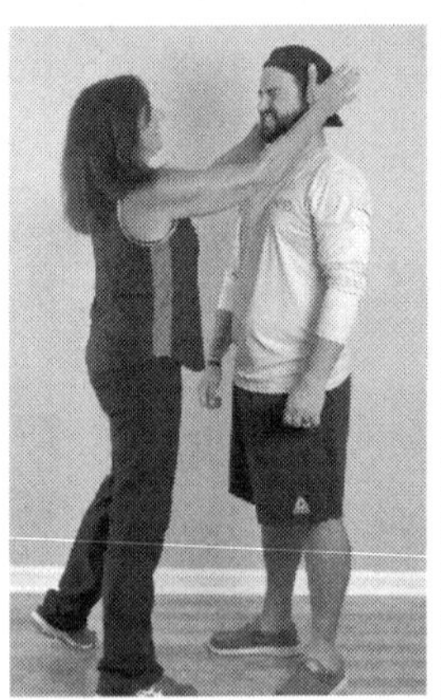

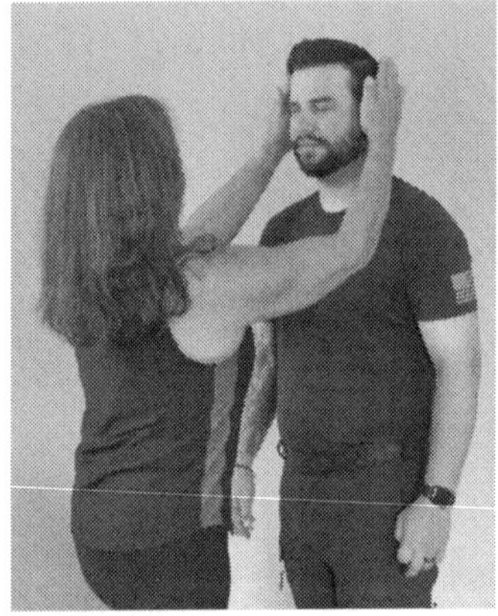

*Ears*

Drive your open hand or firmly locked fingers into their throat.

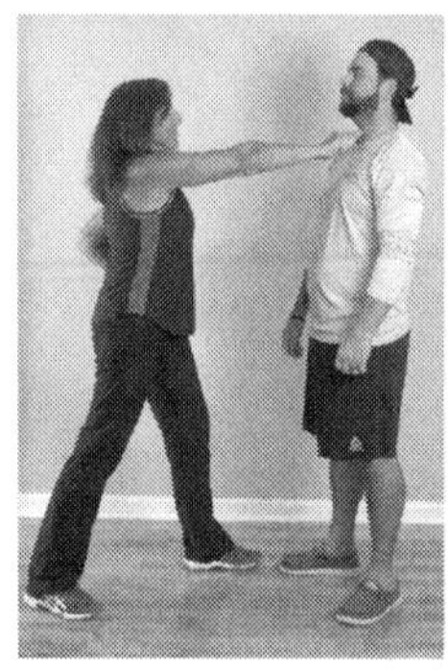 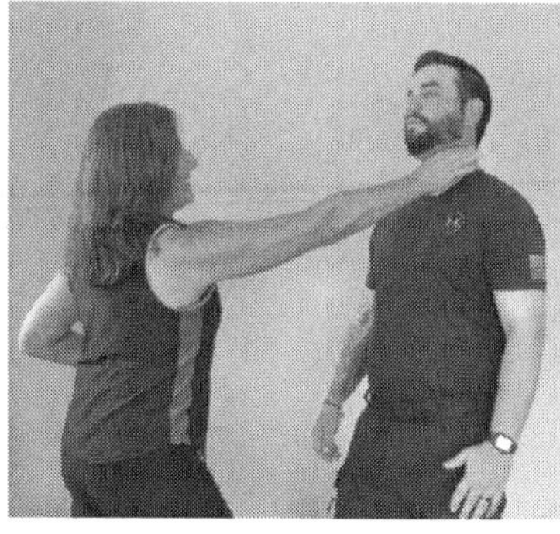

*Throat*

Here, I am driving my knee into his groin area. To get more force, I am placing my hands on his shoulders to bring him closer to me. You can use a knee, foot or fist.

*Groin*

Disable a knee with a kick on the lateral side of the leg. This makes the knee buckle in and causes pain.

*Knee*

**Strikes**:

- Punch
- Elbow
- Kicks
- Knee

Self-defense involves using techniques to protect yourself in dangerous situations. Here are some basic self-defense strikes that can help you defend against an attacker.

To initiate power when striking, we need to exhale as we strike!

In practicing the following physical techniques, you must exhale to create power from your "Chi." Chi is an energy current that passes through the body, physical objects, and the space around us. We use Chi in martial arts to build power and speed.

If the client gets physical with you when they are off the table, we need to defend ourselves in a more physical manner. In order to physically defend ourselves, one thing we need to keep in mind is the importance of breathing. As we perform a technique, we should exhale on the exertion.

Here are a few examples of proper breathing:

- You can hear a professional tennis player exhale (or even grunt) as they are striking the ball.
- Martial Artists are trained to "KiUp" as they strike.
- Weight lifters train to exhale on the exertion.
    - During a bench press, they exhale as they push the bar up.
- Yoga practitioners exhale with the intention of getting a deeper stretch.
    - The Sanskrit word for "exhale" is "rechaka."
- A massage therapist uses their exhaled breath on the forward movement of their stroke.

Besides proper breathing, it is very important to use our legs and core muscles to generate power.

**Strikes:**

**1. Straight punch (jab or cross):**

- One of the most basic strikes, delivered with the fist. A jab is quick, and a cross is thrown with more power.
- A jab is aimed at the opponent's face, eyes, or nose, while a cross follows up with a punch to the same target.

**2. Elbow strike:**

- A powerful close-range strike using the elbow. It is particularly effective in tight situations when you can't throw a full punch.
- Aim for the opponent's face, ribs, or stomach.

**3. Palm heel strike:**

- A safer alternative to a punch, especially if you have weak wrists or hands.
- Strike with the heel of your palm, aiming at the nose, chin, or jaw.

**4. Knee strike:**

- Used at close range, especially when an attacker is near your body.
- Strike with your knee to the opponent's abdomen, groin, or lower ribs.

**5. Front kick:**

- A quick, powerful kick aimed at the opponent's torso or groin.
- You can deliver the kick with the ball of your foot to push your attacker away or cause pain.

**6. Roundhouse kick:**

- A kick delivered with the shin or the top of the foot to the side of your attacker's head, torso, or knee.
- It's effective for striking from a distance or when they are at your side.

**7. Backfist:**

- A quick strike using the back of your fist.
- It's used in situations where you can't punch directly, but you need to hit with a sudden, unexpected motion.

## Where the Head Goes, the Body Follows!

Using the palm heal strike, place the heel of the hand under the chin and push it up and away!

These pictures demonstrate that when I used a palm heel strike and pushed on my son's jaw, his body fell the way I pushed.

A punch is with a straight arm and wrist. Your goal is to strike using your first two knuckles on your target.

*Punch*

To strike with an elbow, use your opposite hand to force your elbow into them.

*Elbow strike*

The palm heel strike drives the base of the nose with force upward and into the head.

*Palm strike*

The knee strike can be driven into any target area. Get more force by bringing your target to your knee.

*Knee strike*

The front kick is a strong push using the ball of your foot.

*Front kick*

The round kick gets a lot of power using your hips as you rotate on your standing leg. The strike is with the top of your foot or shin.

*Round kick*

Using the back of your fist, drive through the nose or any area of the head.

*Backfist*

**Tips for effective self-defense:**

- **Stay relaxed:** Tension can slow you down and make your strikes less effective.
- **Use your environment:** Defend yourself using nearby objects, like keys, a purse, or a chair, if necessary.
- **Aim for vulnerable areas:** Attack the eyes, nose, throat, groin, or knees.
- **Keep distance when possible:** If you can escape or create space, do so.

These techniques are foundational, but training with a qualified instructor (such as in Krav Maga, Brazilian Jiu-Jitsu, or other martial arts) is the best way to build confidence and effectiveness in self-defense.

Escaping a grab or hold depends on the type of grip and the situation. Here are several general techniques that can help you break free:

**1. Stay calm and assess:**

- **Stay composed:** Panicking can make it harder to think clearly. Breathe deeply, and quickly assess the position of the person holding you and the nature of the grab.

**2. Escape a wrist grab:**

- **Twist and pull:** The best way to escape a wrist grab is to twist your wrist toward the thumb (the weakest point of the grip). This takes advantage of the natural direction of your hand and weakens their hold.
- **Step back and pull away:** While twisting, take a step back and pull your hand toward your body. This can destabilize the person holding you.

**3. Escape from a bear hug (arms around the body):**

- **Low bear hug (around the waist):** If your attacker is grabbing you around the waist and lifting or pinning you, drop your weight low.
  - o **Drop your hips:** Lower your center of gravity and squat slightly. This makes it harder for the person to lift you.
  - o **Rear elbow strike:** Use your elbows to strike backward, aiming at the attacker's head, chest, or abdomen.
  - o **Foot stomp or knee strike:** Stomp or knee them in the shin or groin to cause discomfort and create space.

- **High bear hug (around the chest):**
    - o **Move your arms quickly:** Try to break their grip by bringing your hands together in front of you and using them to push against their arms.
    - o **Headbutt or elbow:** A headbutt to their face or an elbow strike to their ribs can create an opening for escape.
    - o **Leg sweep or trip:** If you're balanced, a low leg sweep or knee to their lower leg can help destabilize them.

**4. Escape from a chokehold:**

- **Use your hands:** If someone is choking you with one or both hands, use your hands to push or pull their arm off your neck. Focus on their wrist or forearm to create a gap for airflow.
- **Tuck your chin:** Lower your chin to your chest to reduce the pressure on your throat. This gives you more time to react.
- **Sideways escape:** Twist your body and move to the side. Use your elbow to push their arm away while trying to rotate out of the hold.
- **Create space:** Push their arm down with one hand, and with your other hand, strike or push them away to create space.

**5. Escape from a headlock (side neck grab):**

- **Tuck your chin and protect your neck:** Always keep your chin tucked to protect your neck and airway.

- **Use your hands:** Place your hands on the attacker's arm and push away or pull it to create space.
- **Turn and use your body:** Rotate your body toward the arm that's around your neck and attempt to throw off the attacker's balance.

**6. Escape from a full nelson (both arms behind your head):**

- **Duck your head:** Tuck your chin and try to lower your body weight to make it harder for them to hold you.
- **Use your hands:** Bring your hands to their arms to pry them off or create space.
- **Pivot or twist your body:** Rotate your body and use your legs to push away from the person holding you.

**7. Escape from a collar or lapel grab:**

- **Use leverage:** Grab their arm or wrist and try to push it away while stepping back to increase distance.
- **Strike vulnerable areas:** If they're holding your collar or lapel, you can strike them with a knee to the groin, elbow to the face, or use a quick uppercut.

**8. General principles:**

- **Focus on weak points:** Eyes, throat, groin, and knees are weak spots on most people. A quick strike to these areas can create an opportunity for escape.
- **Use your body weight:** When trying to escape a hold, use your body weight to unbalance or leverage your way out. Try not to use too much brute force if you can use technique.

- **Move unpredictably:** Making sudden, unpredictable movements can surprise your attacker and give you a chance to break free.

Remember that these techniques can vary depending on the strength and positioning of the person holding you, as well as the environment you're in. Training in self-defense or martial arts (such as Krav Maga, Brazilian Jiu-Jitsu, or Muay Thai) can give you more confidence and improve your ability to escape a variety of holds.

## Wrist Escape

*The hold*

*Make a fist and lift your thumb*

*Rotate your hands toward the opening of their hand, and lift your arm and pull out quickly*

## Bear Hug from the Back

*Back bear hug* *Headbutt*

*Groin punch*

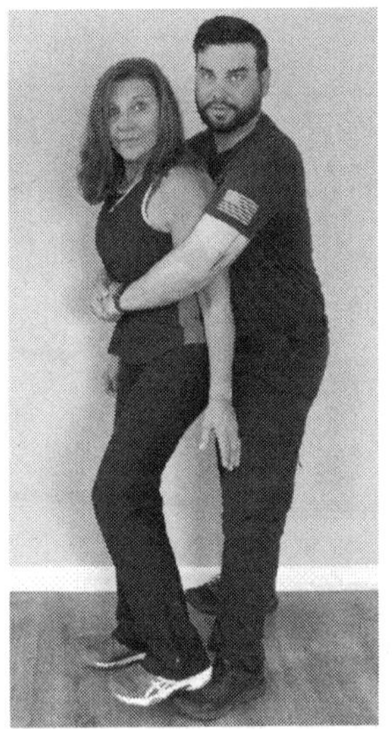
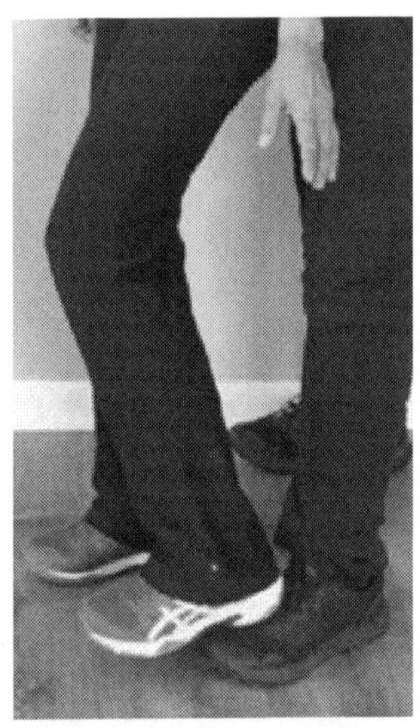

*Heal stomp*

Using your knuckles, "knock" on the back of the hand and rub up and down very hard.

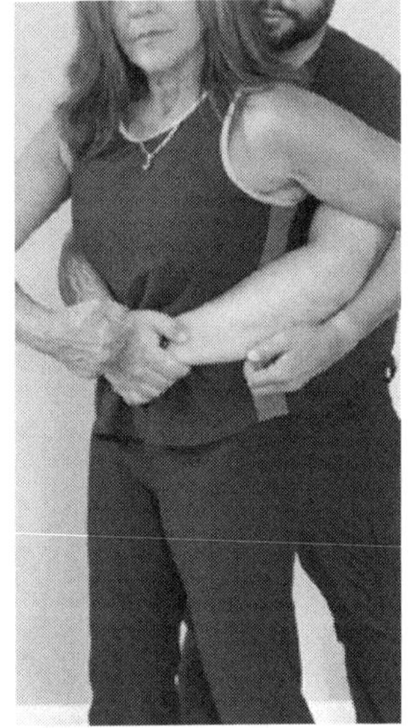

*Door knocker*

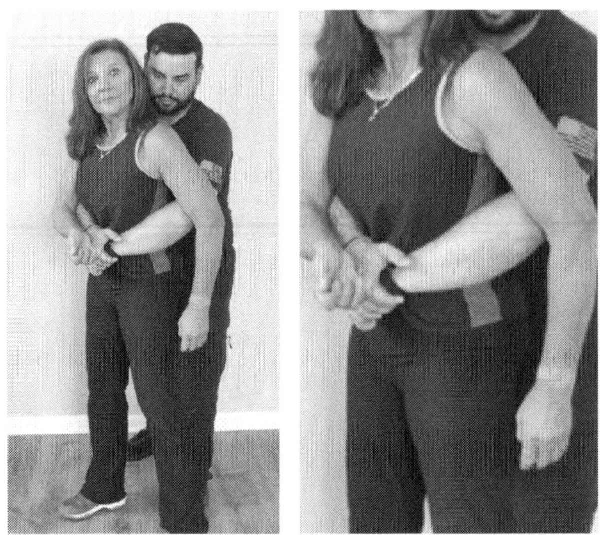

*Finger grab and rip it away*

## Front Bear Hug

*Front bear hug*

*Place thumbs inside their hips*

*Drop your hips and push them back*

*Get away*

## Choke Hold from Front

*Choke hold*

*Drop your hips and bring your hands together*

*Raise your arms up fast through theirs, then separate them (think "Field Goal")*

# Head Lock

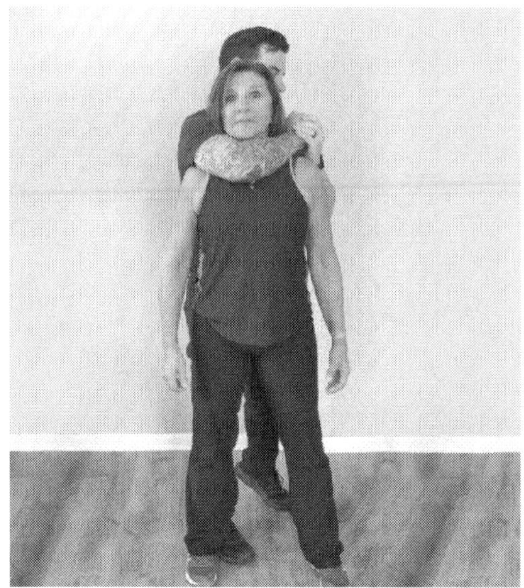

*Head lock*

*Drop your chin while making space at their elbow so you can breathe. Drop your hips*

*Rotate and bend forward simultaneously*

## Lapel Grab with Arm Hold

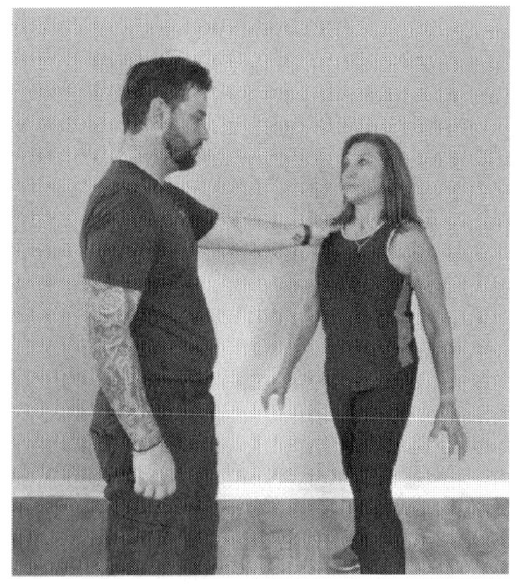

*Lapel grab hold*

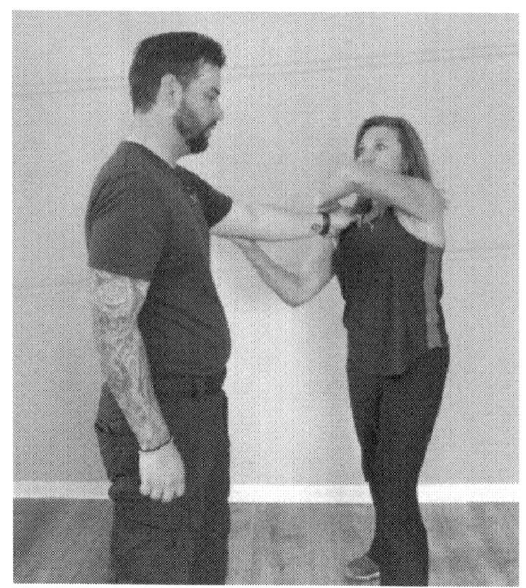

*Place your hand on their elbow while reaching across their hand*

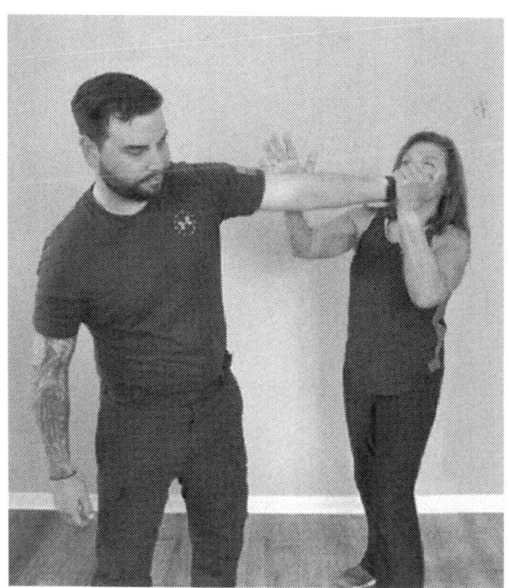

*Put pressure on their elbow and bend their wrist*

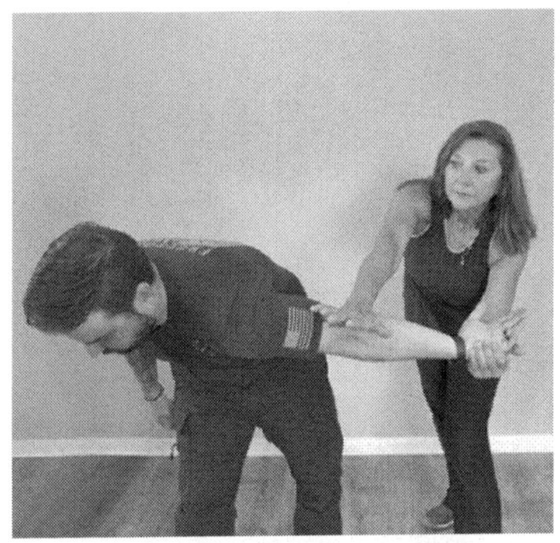

*Push the elbow while controlling the hand/wrist*

## Lapel Grab with Push Away

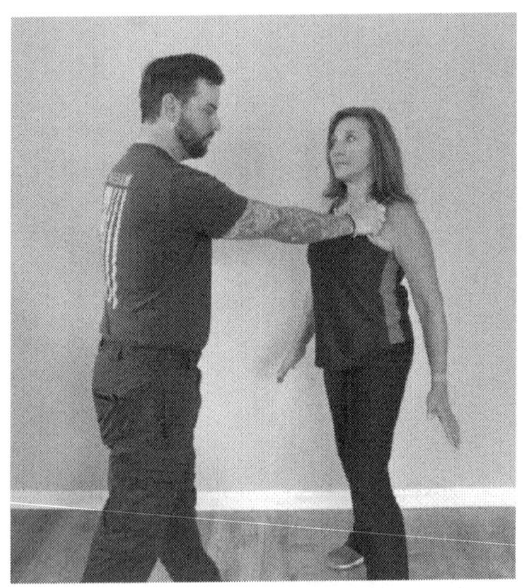

*Lapel grab push*

*With both hands, grab their wrist and bend it back*

*With a firm grip on their hand with their wrist bent, push them back*

# Loud N' Proud

**Don't be afraid to be vocal.** If someone is following you and making unwanted verbal contact (cat calls, harassment, etc.), make a scene that turns the discomfort on them, ultimately causing them to leave. This may be especially important if it is nighttime in a residential neighborhood. You need to get people looking out their windows or opening doors to see what's happening. Stay in a well-lit area so people can see you. Run up to somebody's porch and get under the porch light if you have to.

**If possible, get into a high-visibility public location as quickly as possible.** Make sure other people can see you and your harasser clearly. Surround yourself with witnesses and potential allies.

**Say loudly and firmly, "I don't know this person and s/he is harassing me."** Don't shy away from using the simple phrase **"I need help."**

Your would-be-attacker probably isn't prepared to deal with an audience, and will usually abandon ship right there. Within any crowd, there is at least one person who will recognize the situation for what it is. This person may choose to create a physical barrier between you and the harasser. They may also vocalize that the harasser is not welcome and should leave, or even suggest calling the police. Once you have someone else standing with you, it doesn't take much before a would-be-attacker decides you aren't worth the trouble. Remain in the company of others until you are confident the harasser is gone.

You may find yourself in a location where an audience is not readily available. Do not verbally engage the person harassing you unless they make a move to approach or you feel in immediate danger. **If they start toward you, scream and yell so that people in the area might hear you and look out their windows.** Yell the phrases above, or make it very clear that contact isn't welcome with a firm, loud "BACK OFF!" or "GO AWAY!" *Be firm. Commit and do not waver or sound unsure.*

**Attackers target people who they perceive will be weak in the moment and an easy target. Being loud and making a scene tells them you will not go quietly. It throws them off their game and often causes them to abandon the attack. Your goal is to remain safe and get away unharmed!**

**What would you do?**

*Shelly, a female therapist, new to the profession, revealed to me she has a client who constantly asked her very personal questions as she massages him. When asked how that made her feel, she said "extremely uncomfortable." The questions ranged from "Are you married?," "Do you have kids?," "Where do they go to school?," and "Where do you live?"*

*Find out what Shelly did in Chapter 10.*

CHAPTER 8

# Self-Care: Physical Capabilities

As the previous chapter demonstrated, most defensive tactic skills require physical fitness, strength, balance, and flexibility.

This chapter could be an entire book in itself! It will cover some stretching, strength training, core and balance, and endurance training. Of course, there is more to "self-care" than this chapter identifies. To name a few: proper nutrition (add more whole foods: fruits and vegetables, limit sugar and processed foods, etc.), stress reduction, proper sleep, water intake, getting your steps in, time off, and getting a massage. All these components of self-care will help us meet our goals to be a better version of ourselves.

As certified personal trainers, our goal is to encourage you to make self-care part of your lifestyle. We need a certain amount of physical ability if we have a physically demanding job, or if we are in a situation where we need to defend ourselves. Some results of having greater strength and physical power can boost your self-confidence, ease your day-to-day activities, prevent injury, improve your posture, and improve your appearance. Muscular strength and muscular endurance, stretching and flexibility, and lastly, balance training and core strength are the aspects of fitness that identify our physical being.

We will share with you some of our favorite stretches, strength training exercises, balance, and core exercises you can do regularly. Even if you are new to exercise or are adding these to your current routine, you will become stronger and more flexible, which will allow you to manage everyday activities with greater ease. By also adding some endurance exercises, you will enhance all the above! Doing these regularly may also give you more confidence because you will feel stronger and healthier.

No two people are the same when it comes to any exercise or activity. There are a range of factors, such as—age, gender, heredity, physical capability, or physical issues. As a reminder, before you perform any of the following exercises, be sure to consult with your healthcare provider. Do not strain or go beyond your physical limitations. Modified versions are available if you need to alter a technique.

There may be exercises that are in the stretching or strength training section, and you might feel they are working your balance or endurance—that is a bonus! Stretching, strength training, core/balance, and (cardio) endurance should be included in your fitness routine to take care of yourself. Personally, we find when done daily, there is a true balance of body, mind, and spirit.

# Self-Care: Being Mentally and Physically Prepared

One of my favorite quotes is from MLB player Mickey Mantle: "If I knew I was going to live this long, I would have taken better care of myself."

Let's take a deeper look at this quote. Allowing our physical body to go through our daily activities with as much ease as we can, and returning home safely to our family should be a priority. It will allow us to age like fine wine!

We've had a passion for being fit and strong all our lives and wish to be healthy, strong, and able to do everyday activities for a very long time. We also believe it comes down to our habits, lifestyle, and willingness to step outside of our comfort zone. This should be not only for ourselves, but for our family.

Most defensive tactics skills require a certain amount of physical fitness: strength, agility, balance, flexibility, and endurance. Not only will this chapter help you prepare when faced with a situation, but it will also help you become a better version of yourself for everyday life! Our determination and discipline to achieve being fit and strong is where we need to focus.

The different categories are extremely important. Being physically capable of giving the best effort to defend yourself, along with being in great physical shape, will assist us to live a long, healthy, and great quality of life. Strength training and stretching with flexibility exercises allow us to reduce the risk of injuries and a healthy lifestyle in order to be here for our families! That is what we are doing as we learn how to combat unacceptable and unwanted behavior, allowing ourselves to get home safely to our families!

Keep in mind that what we are sharing here is a small sample of things you can do. It is certainly a great place to start!

Going through the following exercises, please start slow and go at a pace that is good for you. When you are doing any of the following, you want to exhale on the exertion. For example, when stretching your hamstring, exhale when you are flexing your hips, or when doing a pushup, exhale on the "up." If you have a physical barrier and an exercise is too strenuous, please consult an expert to see how you can make proper accommodations.

## Stretching

Stretching offers many benefits for both physical and mental well-being:

1. **Improved flexibility:** Regular stretching increases the range of motion in your joints, which can enhance overall flexibility.
2. **Increased blood flow:** Stretching promotes circulation, delivering more oxygen and nutrients to your muscles.
3. **Reduced muscle tension:** Stretching can help relieve tension and stiffness in muscles, leading to a more relaxed feeling.
4. **Enhanced performance:** Stretching can improve performance by preparing muscles for activity and reducing the risk of injury.
5. **Better posture:** Stretching helps to balance muscle groups, which can improve alignment and posture.

6. **Pain relief:** Stretching can ease discomfort caused by tight muscles and may help in managing chronic pain conditions.
7. **Stress relief:** Stretching can be a form of relaxation, helping to reduce stress and anxiety levels.
8. **Improved coordination:** Increased flexibility can enhance body awareness and coordination.
9. **Prevention of injuries:** Regular stretching can help prevent injuries by preparing muscles for physical activity.
10. **Enhanced recovery:** Stretching can aid in recovery after exercise by reducing soreness and promoting muscle repair.

Incorporating stretching into your routine can lead to long-term benefits for your physical health and overall well-being.

As you stretch, synchronize your breathing: exhale on the stretch.

**Some stretches to add to your routine:**

*Hand over head, reach up and over, or hold wrist and stretch laterally*

*Lateral neck stretch: ear to shoulder*

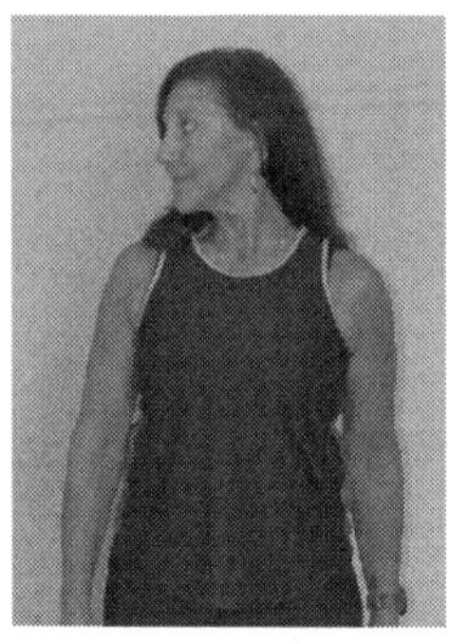

*Rotation neck stretch*

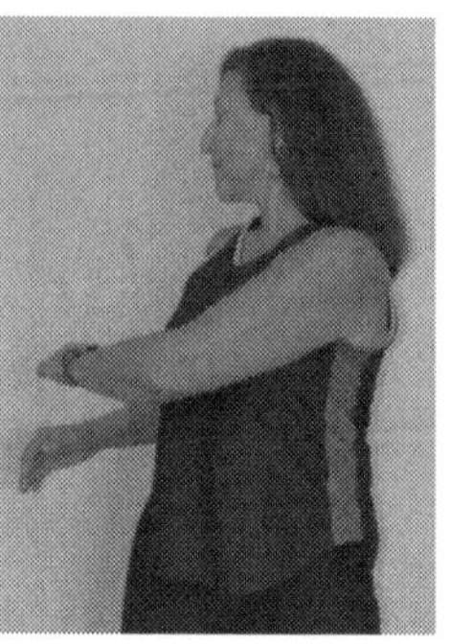

*Trunk rotation*

*Shoulder girdle stretch*

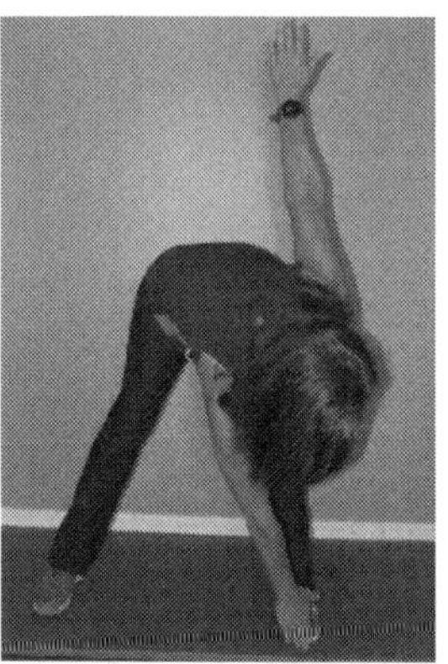

*Wide base, hand to opposite toes*

*Dynamic hamstring: Standing, arms out; straight leg /Toes to opposite hand*

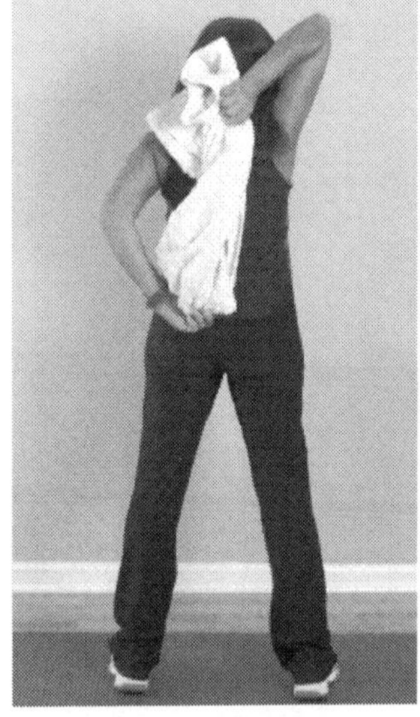

*Triceps stretch: without and with a towel—good ROM for the shoulder too*

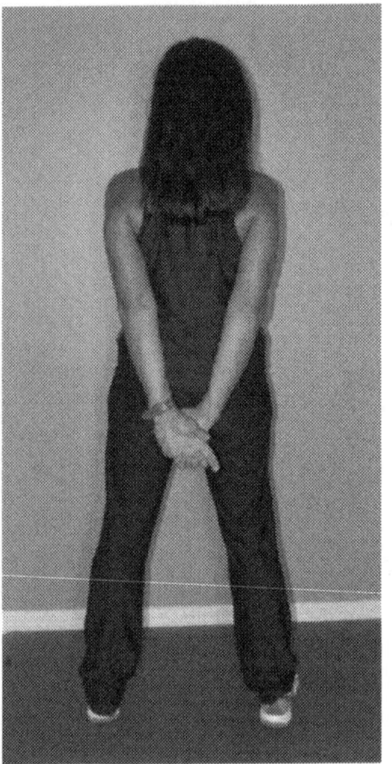

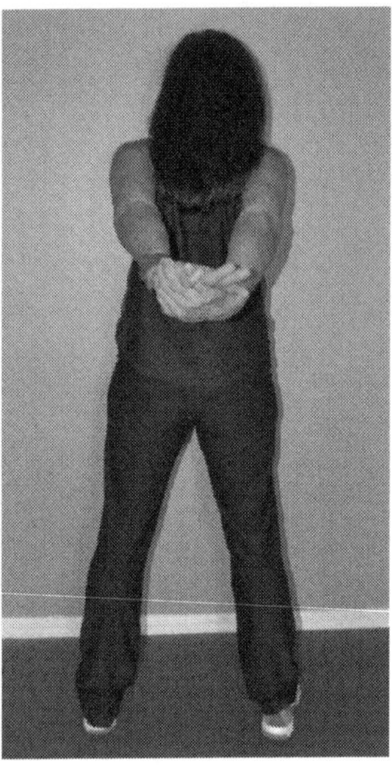

*Pec stretch: lace hands behind back and lift*

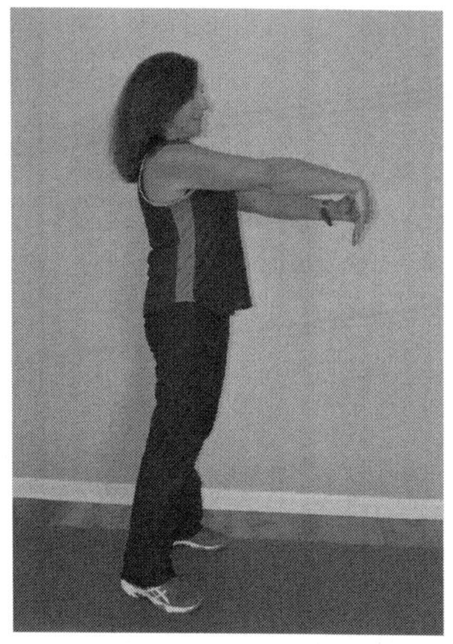

*Forearm extensors*

*Forearm flexors*

*Adductor stretch sitting*

*Adductor stretch standing*

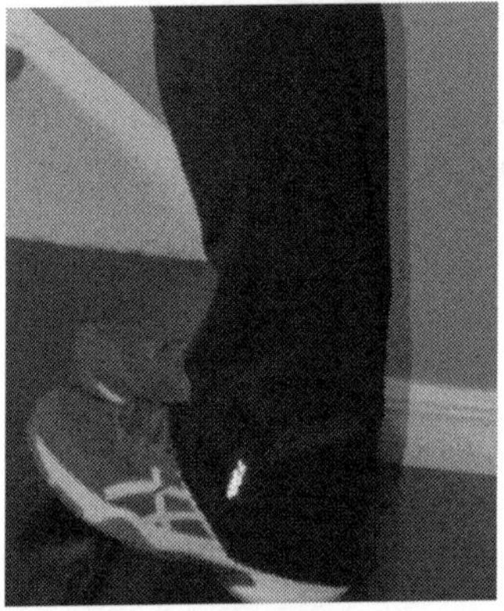

*Calf stretch: Standing on a step and letting your heels drop*

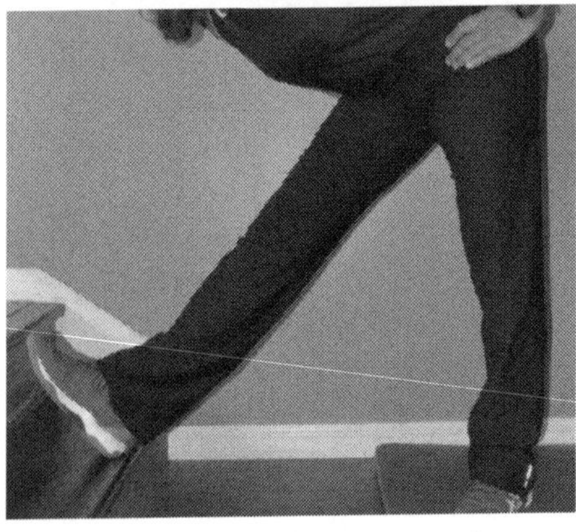

*Standing hamstring stretch 1: put your foot on a step or chair and bring your chest toward your toes*

*Hamstring stretch 2: Sitting on the floor—keep both legs straight, and with a flat back, reach for your toes*

*Hamstring stretch 3: Laying on your back, use a towel to pull your leg up*

*Figure 4 piriformis stretch: On back*

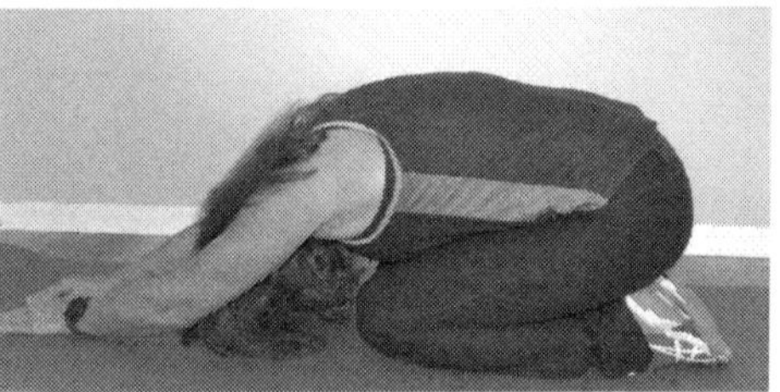

*Child's pose: back stretch*

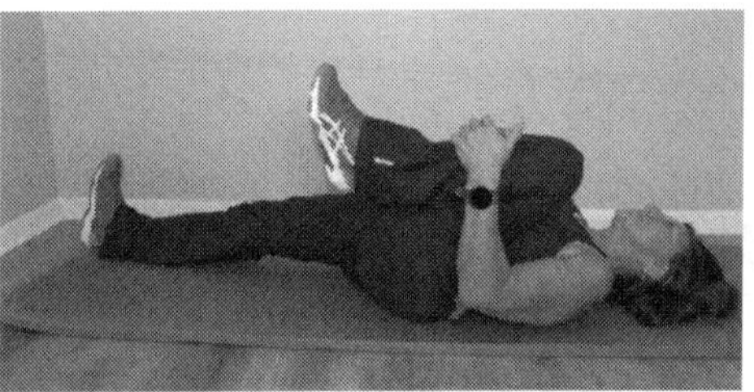

*Quad stretch*

*Knee to chest—on your back*

*Knee to chest standing, you are also working on your balance*

*Torso twist sitting*

*Drop both knees to the left and then right while lying, keeping your shoulders on the floor*

*Hip flexor—on one knee, drive your hips forward, keeping your back straight*

## Strength Training

Strength training offers a wide range of benefits for physical health, mental well-being, and overall quality of life:

1. **Increased muscle strength:** Regular strength training enhances muscle strength and endurance, making everyday activities easier.
2. **Improved bone density:** It helps increase bone density, reducing the risk of osteoporosis and fractures.

3. **Weight management:** Strength training boosts metabolism, helping with weight loss or maintenance by increasing lean muscle mass.
4. **Enhanced joint health:** Stronger muscles support joints, reducing the risk of injury and alleviating joint pain.
5. **Better posture:** Strengthening core and back muscles can improve posture and reduce the risk of back pain.
6. **Boosted mental health:** Exercise, including strength training, releases endorphins, which can improve mood and reduce symptoms of anxiety and depression.
7. **Increased functional strength:** Strength training enhances functional movements, making daily tasks easier and improving overall quality of life.
8. **Improved athletic performance:** It enhances performance in sports by increasing strength, power, and endurance.
9. **Enhanced balance and stability:** Strength training can improve balance, reducing the risk of falls, especially in older adults.
10. **Long-term health benefits:** Regular strength training is associated with a lower risk of chronic diseases, such as heart disease, and diabetes.

Incorporating strength training into your routine can lead to significant improvements in both physical and mental health.

**Some Strength training exercises you can add to your routine:**

- Bicep curls—this is an isometric contraction using one hand as the "weight" and pushing down on other forearm for resistance.

- Triceps extension isometric exercise

- Triceps extension—with resistance band

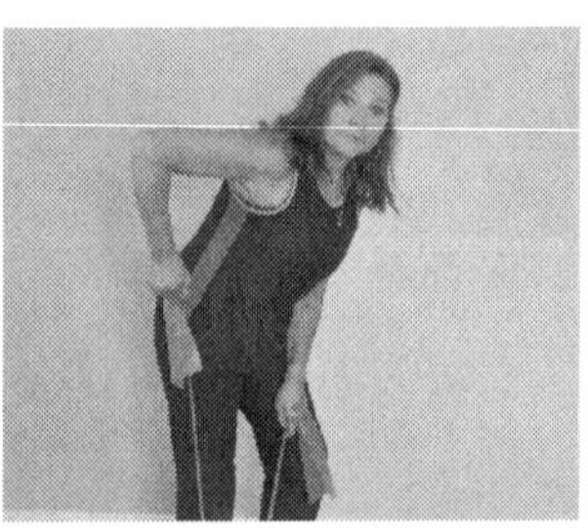

- Hand trainers with a squishy ball

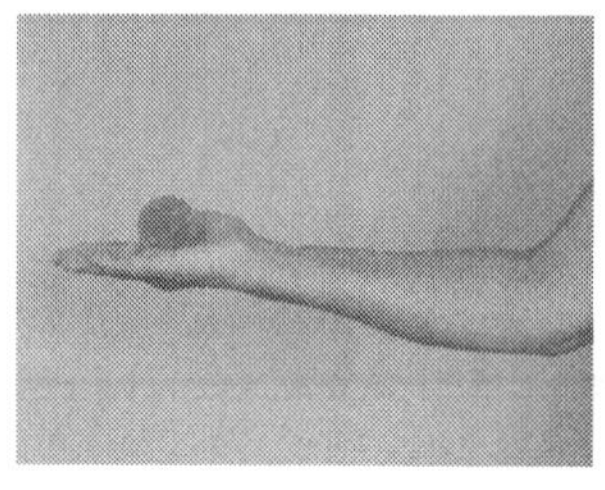
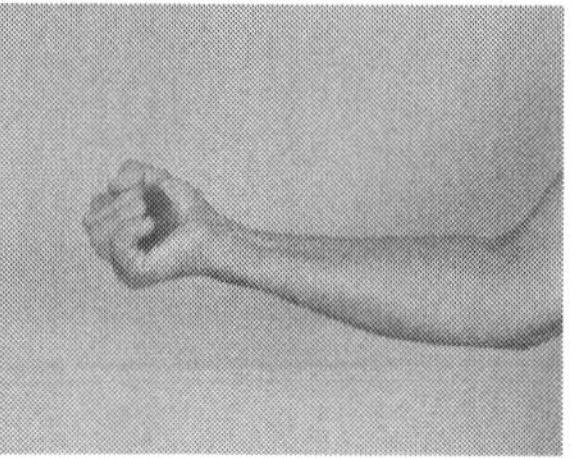

- Anterior raises—with resistance band

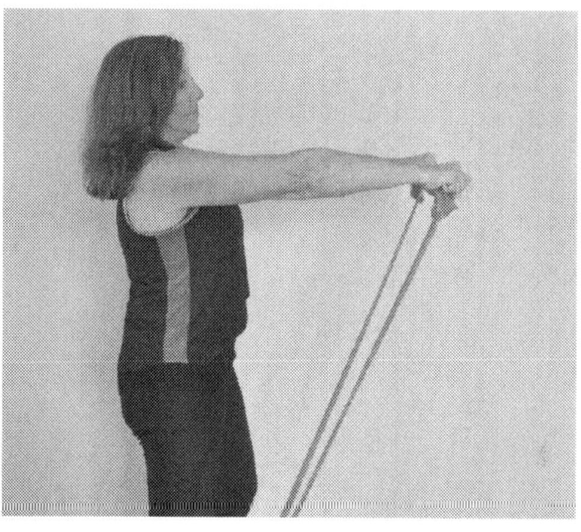

- Lateral raises—with resistance band

- Lat pull downs—with resistance band

- Lunge

- Squat

- Wall squat

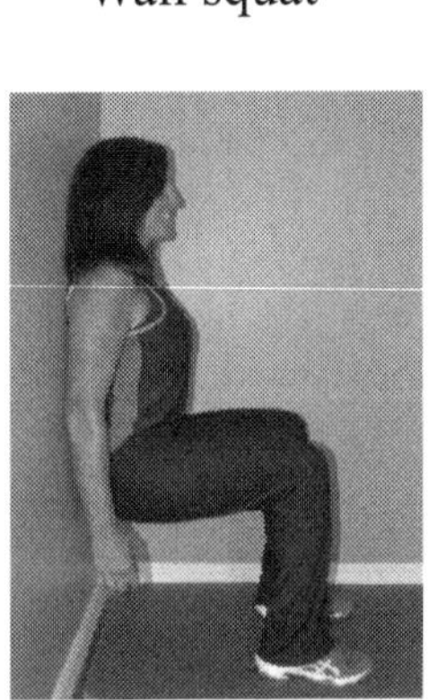

- Curtsy lunge

- Horse stance with alternating punches

- Glute bridge

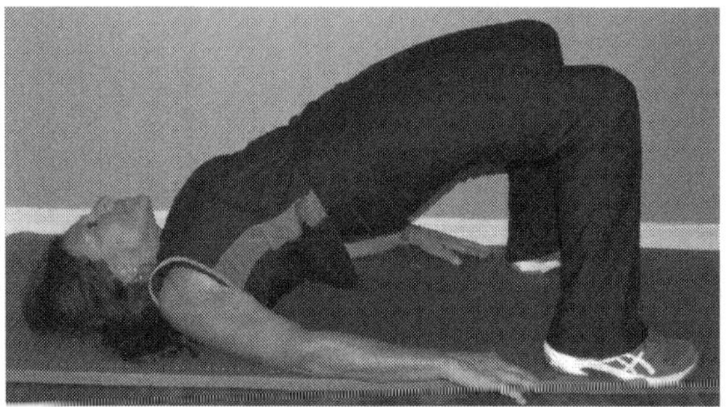

- Leg extension

- Leg lifts-lying down

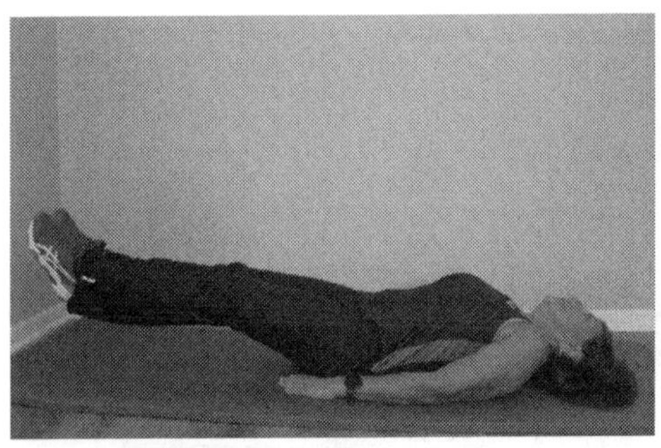

- Push-ups

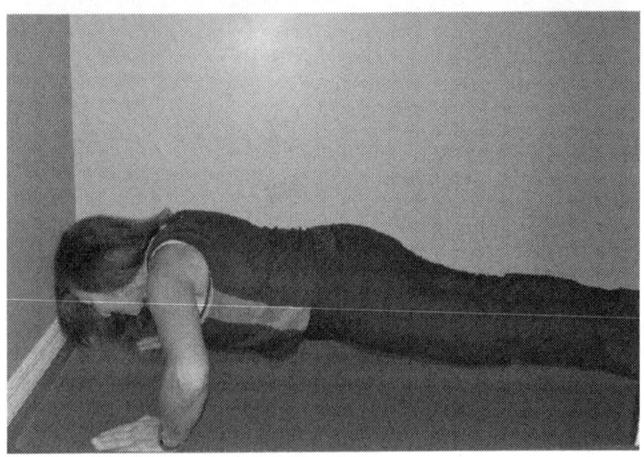

- Vertical scissors

## Core Training and Balance Training

Incorporating core and balance training into your fitness routine can lead to significant improvements in overall strength, stability, and an improved overall quality of life. This training helps improve proprioception (the sense of body position), which is crucial for balance, especially in older adults. Balance training offers a variety of benefits that contribute to overall physical fitness and functional performance. On the other hand, core training provides various benefits that can enhance overall physical health and performance. Here are some key advantages:

1. **Improved stability and balance:** A strong core enhances stability, helping with balance and coordination during various activities and reducing the risk of falls.
2. **Better posture:** Strengthening core muscles supports proper alignment and posture, reducing the risk of back pain and discomfort.

3. **Injury prevention:** By improving balance and stability, core training can help prevent injuries by stabilizing the spine and pelvis, particularly in the lower back, hips, and knees.
4. **Functional strength:** Core training focuses on the muscles used in daily movements, making everyday tasks easier and reducing fatigue. Many balance exercises engage core and leg muscles, contributing to overall strength development.
5. **Mental focus:** Balance training often requires concentration and body awareness, which can enhance mental focus and mindfulness.
6. **Functional strength:** Core exercises improve functional strength, making everyday tasks easier, such as lifting, bending, and twisting, and reducing fatigue.
7. **Better breathing:** Core exercises can help with diaphragmatic breathing, improving lung capacity and overall respiratory function.
8. **Enhanced body awareness:** Core training fosters greater body awareness and control, improving overall movement efficiency.
9. **Enhanced coordination:** Promotes better coordination between different body parts, improving overall movement efficiency. Athletes benefit from a strong core, as it contributes to more powerful movements and better control during activities.
10. **Support for daily activities:** Improves functional strength, making everyday tasks like climbing stairs or carrying groceries easier and safer.

11. **Increased confidence:** Developing balance can boost confidence in physical abilities, encouraging participation in more activities.

Incorporating core and balance training into your fitness routine can lead to significant improvements in stability, strength, and overall physical health.

**Some Core and Balance exercises you can add to your routine:**

- Alternating heel presses

- Plank (On forearms)

- On hands (push-up position)

- Side plank

- Crunches

- Leg lifts

- Russian twists

- Arms up in 90º, standing, raise the knee to the opposite elbow

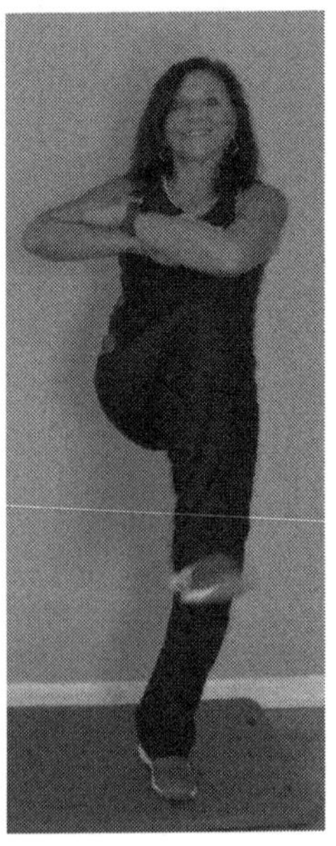

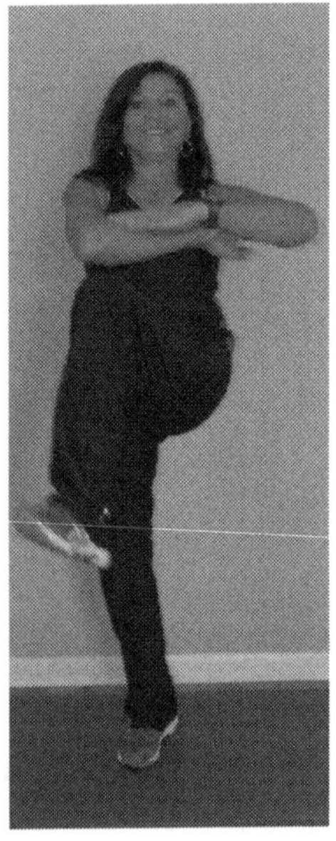

- Standing rotation with resistance band

- Standing Superman

- Table top Superman

## Cardio and Muscle Endurance

Cardio and muscle endurance refers to the ability of a muscle or group of muscles to sustain repeated contractions or maintain a prolonged level of force over an extended period. It is a key component of physical fitness and is essential for activities that require stamina and prolonged effort, such as running, cycling, swimming, performing daily tasks like carrying groceries, or even defending yourself when physically assaulted. Muscle and cardio endurance allow you to perform repetitive movements without quickly tiring out.

### *Cardio Endurance Training*

If you were to get into an altercation, how long do you think you can maintain your energy? You may have the strength and confidence and know what to do, but in the end, you will be saying, "I should have spent more time on conditioning." Cardio

Endurance exercises offer a variety of benefits for overall health and fitness, including:

- **Improved heart health:** Regular cardio strengthens the heart muscle, improving circulation and reducing the risk of heart disease.
- **Increased endurance:** It enhances stamina and endurance, making daily activities easier and less tiring.
- **Weight management:** Cardio is effective for burning calories and can aid in weight loss or maintenance when combined with a balanced diet.
- **Enhanced lung capacity:** Cardio improves respiratory function and increases lung capacity, promoting better oxygen intake.
- **Boosted mood:** Engaging in cardio releases endorphins, which can elevate mood and reduce feelings of anxiety and depression.
- **Better sleep:** Regular aerobic exercise can improve sleep quality, helping you fall asleep faster and enjoy deeper sleep.
- **Increased metabolism:** Cardio training boosts the metabolic rate, helping the body burn more calories even at rest.
- **Improved blood sugar control:** It can enhance insulin sensitivity and help manage blood sugar levels, reducing the risk of type 2 diabetes.
- **Enhanced cognitive function:** Cardio is linked to better brain health, including improved memory and cognitive function.

- **Social interaction:** Participating in group cardio activities can provide social benefits, promoting connections and motivation.

Incorporating cardio into your fitness routine can lead to substantial improvements in both physical and mental health.

### *Benefits of muscle endurance training:*

- **Resistance to fatigue:** It helps muscles resist fatigue during prolonged activities, enabling you to maintain performance levels.
- **Improved blood flow:** Training for muscle endurance often enhances circulation, delivering more oxygen and nutrients to the muscles.
- **Increased efficiency:** Better muscle endurance improves overall efficiency in both aerobic and anaerobic activities.
- **Enhanced recovery:** With improved endurance, muscles recover more quickly from exertion.
- **Improved performance:** Essential for athletes in endurance sports and beneficial for general fitness.
- **Injury prevention:** Enhanced endurance can reduce the risk of injuries during physical activities.
- **Functional strength:** Helps with daily activities that require prolonged effort, like climbing stairs or carrying heavy items.
- **Weight management:** Increases overall caloric expenditure, aiding in weight control.

Training for muscle endurance typically involves lower weights and higher repetitions, focusing on exercises that challenge stamina.

Practice the following to the best of your abilities. Stay positive! You will improve daily! Such a type of conditioning will develop:

- Aerobic capacity
- Anaerobic capacity
- Functional strength
- Power
- Muscular, physical, and mental endurance

**Some cardio exercises you can add to your routine:**

- Jumping jacks

- Jump rope

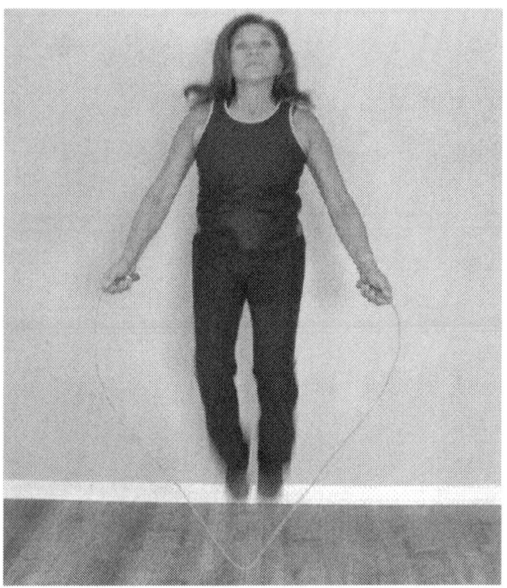

- Jog in place

- Mountain climbers

- Step-ups

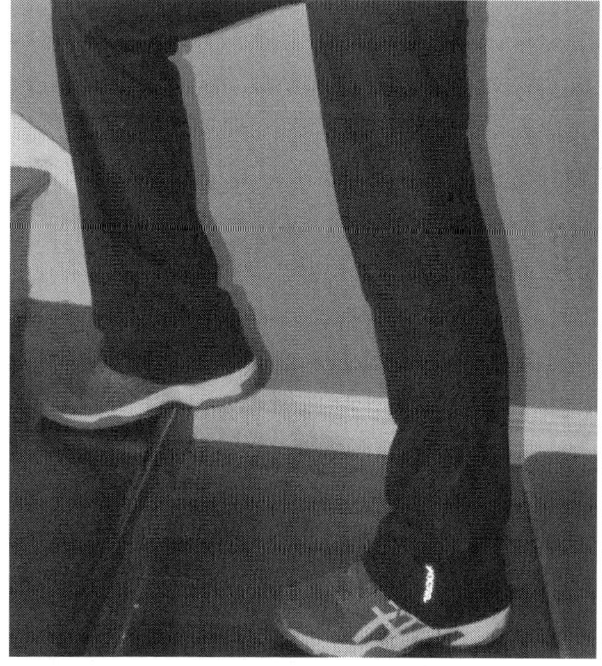

If there was a situation where you had to fight for your life, how long do you think the fight would last? Ten seconds, thirty seconds, one minute, three minutes? When performing the following endurance exercises, start with ten seconds and try to build up to one minute or more.

Shadow box: You can look in a mirror to see yourself as your opponent and pretend to box. Start with ten seconds!

This is Johnny (in the blue trunks) in a Charity Boxing Event: The 2013 Guns n' Hoses (Police vs. Firefighters). Three one-minute rounds were exhausting!

## Shadow Box

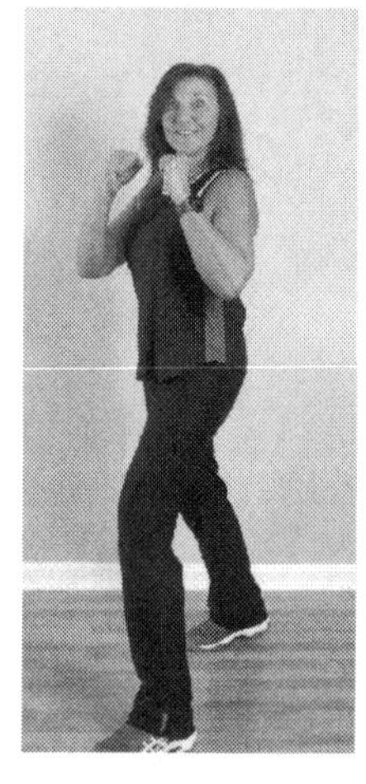

Keep your hands up, use an "athletic stance" with a little bounce, and punch. Alternate hands continuously for thirty seconds!

Next time, try for forty-five seconds. Then challenge yourself to the shadow box for one full minute! Over time, you will continue to build on your endurance.

Once you feel comfortable, you can add something to actually hit.

You can punch a shield, a wave master, or a BOB!

*This is a shield*

*This is BOB! He stays in the backyard and gets kicked and punched every time we walk by him*

This will work your cardio and your shoulders, legs, and core!

We are not as young as we once were, so let's do something so our future selves will be thankful. Self-care is not just about stretching and strength training. Self-care allows us to be strong, flexible, have balance, and endurance to do the best we can if we found ourselves in an altercation.

As mentioned at the beginning of this chapter, it is also about reducing stress in your life, as well as eating healthy. These activities may actually help you relieve some stress and promote better sleep! To include proper eating habits in your daily life, you may wish to consult with a nutrition professional.

**What would you do?**

*Veronica has been a therapist for sixteen years. She also has training in martial arts. One of her regular male clients kept touching her thigh as she moved around the table. The first time it happened, she thought she allowed her body to get too close, so she adjusted her body mechanics. It happened two more times.*

*See what Veronica did in Chapter 10.*

CHAPTER 9

# Be Proactive!

Dealing with inappropriate behavior from a massage client is a serious matter, and it's important to prioritize your safety, professionalism, and well-being. Here are steps you can take to prevent and defend yourself in such situations:

**1. Set clear boundaries:**

- **Before the session:** Establish clear, professional boundaries. Let the client know that the massage is a therapeutic service and any inappropriate behavior is unacceptable. It's also helpful to communicate the scope of the session—such as the areas of the body you'll work on, etc.
- **During the session:** If the client is crossing boundaries, remind them of the professional nature of the session and that you will not tolerate any inappropriate behavior.
- Make sure you use proper draping, giving the client a feeling that the therapist is in control and this is a therapeutic treatment.

**2. Stay calm and professional:**

- If the client starts to act inappropriately, stay calm and keep your voice steady. Avoid reacting emotionally, as that can escalate the situation.
- Maintain professionalism and remind them that you're there to provide therapeutic care, and anything outside of that is not acceptable.

**3. Stop the session if necessary:**

- If the behavior continues or escalates, it may be necessary to stop the session immediately. Politely, but firmly, tell the client that the session will end if they do not respect your boundaries.
- You can say something like: "If this behavior continues, I'll have to end the session."

**4. Document the incident:**

- Write down what happened, including the date, time, and any details that are relevant. If you feel that the behavior is threatening or serious, having documentation can be helpful for any future legal or professional steps.
- Keep a record of any previous incidents as well, if it's an ongoing issue.

**5. Remove yourself from the situation:**

- If you ever feel unsafe, it's important to leave the situation immediately. Trust your instincts.
- Consider asking for help from a colleague, a supervisor, or someone in the area if you need to exit the room or building.

**6. Follow professional protocols:**

- If the inappropriate behavior is severe or threatening, report the incident to your employer (if applicable) or police. They may have protocols for dealing with these situations.
- If you're working independently, you may want to consider reaching out to a legal advisor or local authorities, especially if the situation involves harassment or assault.

**7. Consider client banning:**

- If a client is continually inappropriate or makes you uncomfortable, you may choose to refuse service in the future. Clarify that you do not tolerate any behavior that undermines your professionalism or well-being.

**8. Use personal safety measures:**

- If possible, work in environments with security, cameras, or other safety measures that can help protect you.
- Ensure that someone knows where you are during each session or that your workplace has protocols for checking on employees.

**9. Trust your intuition:**

- Your safety and mental well-being are the most important. If something feels off or uncomfortable, never think twice about removing yourself from the situation and seek help if necessary.
- By maintaining strong boundaries, staying calm and professional, and taking appropriate action when

necessary, you can protect yourself in challenging situations.

## Get Loud and Push Back

As soon as the attacker touches you or it's clear that escape isn't possible, shout loudly ("BACK OFF!") and push back at him or her. It does two things: signals for help and lets the attacker know you're not an easy target. Getting loud will warn off those who are looking for easy prey.

## The Most Effective Body Parts to Hit

When you're in a confrontation, you only have a few seconds and a few moves to try before the fight gets decided. Before an attacker has gained full control of you, you must do everything you can—conserving as much energy as possible—to inflict injury so you can get away. (This is no time to be civil. In a physical confrontation that calls for self-defense, it's hurt or get hurt.) So, aim for the parts of the body where you can do the most damage easily: the eyes, nose, ears, neck, groin, or knee.

- **Eyes:** Gouging, poking, or scratching the attacker's eyes with your fingers or knuckles would be effective, as you can imagine. Besides causing a lot of pain, this should also make your escape easier by at least temporarily interfering with his vision.
- **Nose:** If the attacker is close in front of you, use the heel of your palm to strike up under his nose; throw the entire weight of your body into the motion to cause the most pain and force him to loosen his grip on you. If

he's behind you, you can strike his nose (from the side or the front) with your elbow or head. Either way, aim for the nasal bones.

- **Neck:** The side of the neck is a bigger target, where both the carotid artery and jugular vein are located. You could temporarily stun your attacker with a knife hand strike (all fingers held straight and tightly together, with thumb tucked and slightly bent at the knuckle) at the side of the neck or the front of the neck.
- **Knee:** The knee is an ideal self-defense target, vulnerable from every angle and easily kicked without risk of your foot being grabbed. Kick the side of the knee to cause injury or partially incapacitate your attacker. Kicking the front of the knee may cause more injury, but is less likely to result in imbalance.

**Use your elbows, knees, and head.** These are the parts of the body used most effectively for inflicting damage: your elbows, knees, and head (they're your body's bony built-in weapons).

**Use everyday objects.** Everyday objects you carry around with you or things in your environment can also be used to your advantage as weapons. Outdoors, you can toss some dirt or sand into your attacker's eyes. Women have been told to spray perfume or hairspray into an assailant's eyes. The point is, use whatever you can to strengthen your defense.

**Leverage your weight.** No matter your size, weight, or strength in relation to your opponent, you can defend yourself by strategically using your body and the simple law of physics. This is the principle behind martial arts, where a smaller person can defeat a larger one.

You don't want to be standing there trading punches or kicks with an attacker; in a violent situation, it's critical to injure him/her using efficient, targeted moves. Basically, target those pressure points mentioned in Chapter 7, but leverage your weight to cause the most damage.

## Moves for Getting Out of or Defending Against Common Holds

- **Wrist hold:** Instead of pulling back to try to get out of the hold, squat down into a firm stance and rotate your hand to position your thumb to their thumb. This allows you to remove your wrist from theirs.
- **Front chokehold:** Forcefully, raise your arms to reflect a "field goal."
- **Bear hug:** Drop your weight and try to hit his head with your elbows or stomp his feet with your feet. If that doesn't work, pull his fingers back to force him to release you. (Pulling fingers is also an effective move in a choke hold in some cases.)

## Prevention Is the Best Self-Defense

First, remember that prevention is the best self-defense. Attackers, whatever their objectives, are looking for unsuspecting, vulnerable targets. So be sure to follow general safety tips like "being aware of your surroundings," only walking and parking in well-lit areas, keeping your keys in hand as you approach your door or car, varying your route and times of travel.

Apart from "avoiding confrontation," if you can defuse a situation (talk someone down from physically assaulting you) or "get away"—by handing over your wallet/purse or whatever they want, do that. Hand over your money rather than fight. Nothing you own is worth more than your life!

**Stay strong and healthy**: Practice self-care, include daily exercises and build strength, flexibility, and muscle endurance, and your confidence will also build. Use the "Self-Care" chapter as a guide to get movement in your daily life. The movements shown are good to incorporate any way you can during your day.

For example, do lunges as you walk to your bedroom, or stretch during commercials when you are watching TV. Do you enjoy a challenge? Challenge yourself to see how long you can do certain isometric strength training exercises. Example: For a plank, start out with ten seconds and work your way to forty-five seconds, etc.

What can you do next? Here are a few compelling reasons why everyone should consider learning self-defense:

- **Personal safety:** Knowing self-defense techniques provides the means to protect themselves in potentially dangerous situations. Whether it's a late-night walk home, a solo travel adventure, or even just navigating everyday spaces, having the confidence to defend oneself can make all the difference.
- **Confidence boost:** Learning self-defense isn't just about physical techniques; it's also about mental strength and confidence. Knowing that you have the ability to protect yourself can boost self-esteem and

empower you to assert boundaries in various aspects of life.

- **Prevention and awareness:** Self-defense training often includes lessons on situational awareness and risk assessment. People who undergo such training become more attuned to their surroundings, recognizing potential threats before they escalate. This hands-on approach can help prevent dangerous situations from occurring in the first place.
- **Breaking stereotypes:** Traditionally, women often get portrayed as the weaker sex, perpetuating the notion that they are easy targets for violence. Learning self-defense challenges these stereotypes, demonstrating that women can defend themselves and thus refuse to be victims.

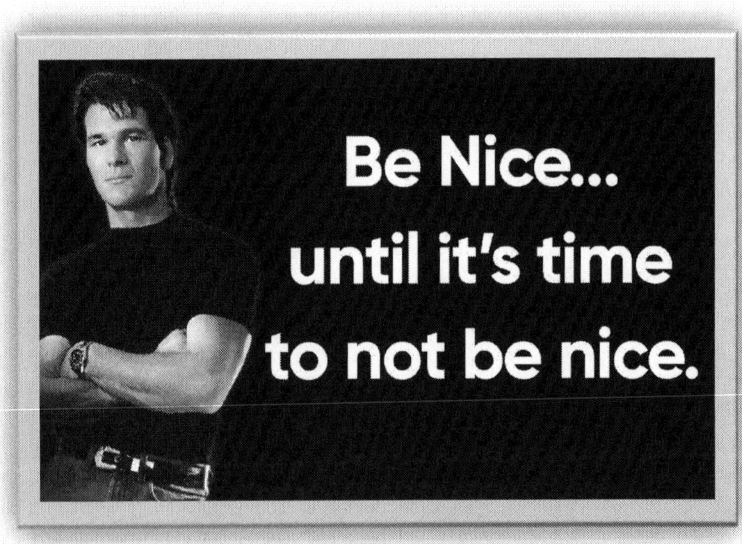

Survival in a criminal assault demands immediate action. The ability to switch from business-as-usual to split-second emergency response depends entirely on having survival decisions—a mindset—already in place.

It is important to play the “what if?” game. Create scenarios in your head and ask yourself, “What if this happens? Where do I go, what do I do, how do I escape? Where are the exits?” Have a plan! Then have a Plan B!

When you work in an unfamiliar environment, identify potential escape routes before beginning the session. Always keep exit doors clear and know where every exit is in your place of business. Let your client know that as part of your professional safety policy, others are aware and nearby.

A therapist carrying a massage table and looking down at her phone on her way to or from her vehicle presents an easier target for criminals.

So, stay alert, and once inside your vehicle, lock the doors and get moving rather than hanging out in the vehicle checking your phone.

Would you be able to defend yourself and your loved ones if someone were to physically attack you? It’s a question most of us don’t want to consider, but violence is, unfortunately, a fact of life. Thankfully, regardless of strength, size, or previous training, anyone can learn several effective self-defense techniques.

Prepare and stay safe in common real-world violent situations.

Many people think of self-defense as a karate kick to the groin or jab in the eyes of an attacker. But self-defense actually means doing everything possible to avoid fighting someone who threatens or attacks you. It's all about using your wisdom—not your fists.

## Color Codes of Awareness

"We must always be aware and live in Condition Yellow!"

The color codes of awareness quantify one's level of mental awareness by assigning a color to how much attention one pays to their surroundings.

- **Condition white:** Unaware or oblivious to your surroundings. *You're texting and looking at your cell phone and you walk into a parked car.*
- **Condition yellow:** Aware of where a potential threat may come from. *In a dark area, shine a light into it or avoid it. If you're walking down the street and a strange-looking person is coming toward you, quickly cross the street.*
- **Condition orange:** Alerted to a potential threat where you might begin to implement your defensive strategy. *When an unsavory person approaches you, your response is to create distance, yell (posture), and/or prepare a defensive tool.*
- **Condition red:** Alarmed to an actual threat that requires you to defend yourself. You're walking in a parking lot at night, and you notice someone acting suspiciously, such as pacing back and forth, eyeing you, and moving toward you quickly. You're aware of the threat and prepare yourself mentally to respond, possibly by

finding an exit route, being ready to defend yourself, or calling for help.

- **Condition black:** When you don't know what to do because you are so frightened, you cannot move. You're caught off guard in a dangerous situation, such as an armed robbery or a sudden violent attack. Your heart is racing, and you're in a complete state of panic, struggling to comprehend what's happening or how to react. You're paralyzed by fear, and your ability to think clearly and act gets severely diminished.

Remember that a simple color system can't always accurately measure our awareness level. Life is never that black and white.

The color code "system" is a good way to introduce people to the concept of paying attention to their surroundings. Using all your senses (including that sixth one) helps you avoid dangerous situations and unsavory individuals and circumstances. It is a brilliant concept and the cornerstone of all defensive curriculums. Situational awareness facilitates conflict avoidance, or anticipation of the need to deploy a defensive tool.

- Protect yourself
- Have situational awareness
- Avoid potential danger
- Practice these tips
- Stay strong, fit, healthy, and safe
- Educate yourself with more training

**"Never fight until you have to. But when it's time to fight, you fight like you're the third monkey on the ramp to Noah's Ark... and brother, it's startin' to rain."**

**What would you do?**

*Eve has been a therapist for twelve years. Her female client, of five years, purchased a massage gift certificate for husband. When the husband came in for his session, he made comments to Eve showing a sexual interest. He actually asked her if she'd like to join him and his wife one evening.*

*Find out what Eve Did in Chapter 10.*

CHAPTER 10

# "What Would You Do?" Results

Find out what the therapist actually did in this chapter. All chapter scenarios have been explained in detail.

## What If This Happened to You? What Would You Do?

### Chapter 1

*Paul treated a female client with back pain. He worked on her back with her prone, then side lying for about twenty minutes. When he turned her supine, she grabbed his hand and placed it between her legs.*

What did Paul do when his female client physically took his hand and placed it between her legs? He could not believe what had just happened! This was a client that he had worked on several times, and nothing like this had happened before.

He abruptly removed his hand from her and told her the session was over, then walked out of the room. When she came out of the room, he told her that was not appropriate and that he could not treat her any longer. She was very embarrassed and apologized.

## Chapter 2

*Cheryl worked on a male client four times over a three-month period. Everything was just fine until his fifth visit. She completed the session and told the male client to take his time getting up and come out of the room when he was ready. As she was walking out the door, he grabbed her arm and pulled her close to him, and kissed her.*

Cheryl could not believe her client had grabbed and kissed her. Thankfully, the session was over. She yelled, "Hey!! What are you doing?" Escaping the wrist grab, she left the room. She was in an establishment with other therapists and had the front desk check him out.

She acted professionally when he wanted to rebook. In front of the receptionist, she politely told him she would not rebook him. He apologized and said, "It will never happen again." Cheryl thanked him for his apology and said that she could not work with him in the future.

## Chapter 3

*Adam, a male therapist and a former Army Ranger of considerable stature, had a male client on his table in a medical facility. The client, while prone, reached up and groped the therapist's inner thigh while moving his hand upward.*

Adam immediately moved away from the table, ended the session, and exited the treatment room. Later, he educated the client on boundaries and defined a therapeutic relationship. The client apologized and continued to be Adam's client.

## Chapter 4

*Julie, an experienced female colleague, accepted an out-call appointment with a male client. As she was setting up her table in the living room of the home, the client approached her from behind, wrapped his arms around her in a bear hug, lifted her up off of her feet, and carried her into the bedroom.*

What did Julie do when her male client bear-hugged her and carried her to the bedroom? Fortunately, she had a presence of mind and a skill set that allowed her to defend herself, escape from the situation, and not be victimized. She got away and left the house without her table or equipment. She called the police and reported him. They escorted her back to the house and got her table and equipment.

## Chapter 5

*Jessica was called to a well-known hotel to a professional soccer player's room. She was setting up her table while the soccer player was in the restroom. Jessica looks up as he comes out of the restroom to see him standing there totally naked.*

Jessica was totally shocked to see a professional athlete naked walking toward her. She froze. He approached her and pushed her onto the bed. She yelled, kicked, and tried to push him off of her, but he was physically stronger than her and held her under him.

Fortunately, housekeeping was walking by as she was yelling. She was so loud that housekeeping knocked and opened the door. Jessica ran out of the room, called the police, and pressed charges against him. This trauma made her leave the profession that she absolutely loved. She did not even want to continue as a therapist in any establishment, no matter how safe it was.

## Chapter 6

*A 6'2" male therapist, Henry, shared he has been working on a female client once a month for nine months. On the next visit, he was ending a two-hour, deep-tissue session with a cranial hold. The female client reached up over her head and sensually caressed Henry's arms.*

Though not physically threatened, the unsolicited and unwanted touch emotionally unsettled Henry. Despite his fifteen years of experience in a clinical setting, he remains disturbed by these incidents. Sadly, he left the massage profession.

## Chapter 7

*Shelly, a female therapist, new to the profession, revealed to me she had a client who constantly asked her very personal questions as she massaged him. When asked how that made her feel, she said, "extremely uncomfortable." The questions ranged from "Are you married?," "Do you have kids?," "Where do they go to school?," or "Where do you live?"*

When we asked Shelly what she did about it, she reluctantly admitted she did nothing because she did not know what to do. She thought he was just making conversation. The questions got very personal and made her feel totally uncomfortable. She knew she shouldn't answer his questions, but she did. She did not think fast enough to deflect the questions or to tell him she didn't share that information with clients.

If a client asks you personal questions, know that this is completely unacceptable. Shelly was lucky that he was just making conversation, and that was as far as it went. Shelly also realized that she needed to reexamine her personal boundaries!

## Chapter 8

*Veronica has been a therapist for sixteen years. She also has training in martial arts. One of her regular male clients kept touching her thigh as she moved around the table. The first time it happened, she thought she allowed her body to get too close, so she adjusted her body mechanics. It happened two more times.*

Veronica gave the male client the benefit of the doubt the first couple of times that his hand touched her. The third time is when she verbally told him it was inappropriate for him to touch her. He did not speak and just kept his hand near her leg.

She took his hand and positioned it where she controlled his hand and arm with a joint manipulation technique. He could not move, as she told him he was not supposed to touch her at all. Veronica gave him verbal notice, but he still did not listen. So, while she had his arm locked against the table, she told him she will leave the room and the massage was over. He then got the message.

## Chapter 9

*Eve has been a therapist for twelve years. Her female client, of five years, purchased a massage gift certificate for her husband. When the husband came in for his session, he made comments to Eve, showing a sexual interest. He actually asked her if she'd like to join him and his wife one evening.*

What did Eve do when her client's husband asked her to be sexual with him and his wife? She was so flabbergasted that she laughed because she thought he was joking. When he explained he was serious, she started shaking. She told the man that she was not interested in that at all.

He then told her it could just be the two of them and not include the wife. Now Eve started getting nauseous. Eve was halfway through the session and wanted to finish it because she needed the income. She completed the session, but with a very uncomfortable feeling and an upset stomach.

When he was leaving, he paid her and told her to call them if she ever changed her mind. Eve did not tell him he could not come back in the future; she just let him leave. Later, she called her massage mentor for guidance. She received advice on professional boundaries and communication to assist any conversation like this in the future. She was also told she should have stopped the session even if he refused to pay.

# Appendix: More Safety Tips

## Avoid Being an Easy Target Everywhere

"Be Safe" is something we always tell our friends and family when they head out. Awareness of our daily habits prepares us to stay safe.

Be in control of your environment:

- **Physical (use the environment for protection):** Lock all gates, doors, and windows.
- **Visual (make everything about you, seen as deterrents):** Confident attitude, assertive body language, remove valuables from sight, video cameras, and motion lights.
- **Situational (be safety conscious):** Be aware, head on a swivel, know the exits, and think ahead. Never put yourself in a position that can compromise your safety.

Someone with criminal intentions often looks for an easy target.

**Are you aware of your surroundings if you are texting while waking?**

Be aware of your surroundings. Who is around you? Are they a potential threat? Do they have a weapon?

Would you think a criminal has a lazy side to them? Would they go after an easy target or someone who is aware of their surroundings and paying attention to what is going on around them? DON'T BE AN EASY TARGET!

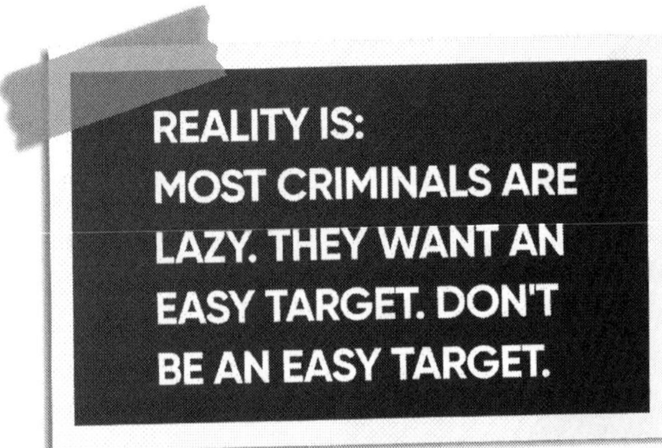

## What Condition of the Color Awareness Chart Are You Living?

Are you in your own world? Are you in Condition White from the Awareness Chart discussed in one of our previous chapters? Meaning, are you thinking of all the things that may have you preoccupied and prevented you from being aware of your surroundings?

"Awareness" can help you avoid danger, give you more time to prepare a response, and serve as a deterrent. Now that is not being paranoid, which is differentiated by irrational fear. We are not afraid—we are just simply aware the world is a potentially dangerous place, and we are prepared to defend ourselves if necessary.

"Remember, if a situation or person feels uncomfortable, leave. If necessary, call for help."

## Safety Tips to Avoid Being an Easy Target

- Pay attention to your surroundings
- Be in the moment
- Avoid distractions, such as your phone, or having your mind wander
- Dress professionally
- Keep your head on a swivel
- Keep hands free so you can defend yourself
- Identify your exits
- Walk confidently

- Speak confidently
- Don't let anyone know you are alone in the facility

It's important to prioritize your safety and stay aware of your surroundings. Here are some practical safety tips to reduce your risk of becoming a target for assault:

- **Stay aware of your surroundings:**
  - o Avoid distractions like looking at your phone while walking, especially in unfamiliar or less-populated areas.
  - o Stay alert and scan your environment for anything or anyone that seems out of place.
- **Trust your instincts:**
  - o If something feels off, trust your gut. Remove yourself from a situation that makes you uncomfortable.
- **Walk in well-lit, populated areas:**
  - o Stick to areas where there are people around, even during the night. Avoid isolated areas, like alleyways or dark streets.
- **Limit alcohol and drug use:**
  - o Excessive alcohol or drug use can impair your judgment and make you more vulnerable. Stay in control of your faculties, especially in unfamiliar settings.
- **Be cautious when accepting help:**
  - o If someone offers assistance, especially in unfamiliar surroundings or situations, assess if it's genuinely

needed or if it might put you in a compromising position.

- **Use safety apps:**
  - Many safety apps allow you to share your location with a trusted friend or alert authorities if you're in danger. Some apps also let you send a distress signal in emergencies.
- **Carry personal protection:**
  - Items like pepper spray, a whistle, or a self-defense keychain can be effective deterrents. Make sure you are familiar and competent with how to use them. Do not carry any self-defense item you have not trained with.
- **Keep your phone charged and accessible:**
  - Always ensure your phone is charged and easily accessible, especially when you're going out. Consider keeping a portable charger if you anticipate being out for a long time.
- **Avoid walking alone at night:**
  - If possible, avoid walking alone at night, especially in areas that feel unsafe. Consider using rideshare services or public transportation instead.
- **Plan your route:**
  - Before heading out, familiarize yourself with the route and alternatives in case you need to change your path. Share your itinerary with a trusted friend or family member.

- **Maintain confidence:**
  - Walk with purpose and confidence. A person who appears unsure or timid may attract attention. Keep your head up, shoulders back, and make eye contact with people around you.
- **Avoid confrontations:**
  - If someone harasses or approaches you threateningly, it's best to stay calm and not engage in confrontation. If possible, create distance and seek help.
- **Secure your belongings:**
  - Keep your valuables close to you. Don't flaunt expensive jewelry or electronics that might attract attention. Use bags that can be securely closed or cross-body bags to deter theft.
- **Learn self-defense:**
  - Taking self-defense classes can help you feel more confident and prepared if you're ever in a dangerous situation. Knowing how to defend yourself physically can be empowering.
- **Know emergency contacts:**
  - Have the contact information for local authorities, close friends, or family members stored on your phone. Additionally, memorize important emergency numbers.

## Safety Tips: While at home

- Have a "Beware of Dog," sign or a "Security System," sign.
- Have cameras.
- Keep weapons in different rooms—baseball bats by the door, knives, guns, hammers, or even spray cleaners. (Keep them away from children.)
- Dogs are a great alarm.
- Do not crack your door open if someone is knocking. It can be forced open easily.
- Check your surroundings before you get out of your car to go into your home.
- Have a deadbolt or more than one lock on your door.
- Make sure to lock and secure all windows and doors before you go to bed.

Here are some things you can do to make your home safer from intruders:

- **Secure doors and windows:** Keep doors locked, even when you're home, and make sure windows have sturdy locks that are used properly. If you live in a vulnerable area, you can add window bars or metal rods to sliding window tracks.
- **Install security systems:** Use a reliable alarm system and security cameras.
- **Use outdoor lighting:** Install effective outdoor lighting, such as yard lighting, to deter criminals. You can also

use light timers to turn your lights on and off at specific times.

- **Trim shrubs and trees:** Burglars like to hide behind shrubs while they pry open windows, so keep shrubs trimmed.
- **Keep your name off mailboxes:** An intruder can use your name on your mailbox or decorative signage to confirm they have the right house.
- **Arrange for mail while you're away:** If you're leaving your home for an extended period, arrange to have your mail held or have a neighbor, friend, or relative retrieve it for you.
- **Educate your family:** Make sure your family knows what to do if someone tries to break into your home.
- **Join a neighborhood watch:** Get to know your neighbors and report suspicious people or vehicles to the police.
- **Use a secure safe:** Keep valuables in a secure safe.
- **Make a list of your valuables:** Keep a list of your valuable property, including serial numbers, and consider engraving or marking them with a personal identifier.
- **Keep photos and videos:** Take photos and/or videotapes of your home and property.
- **Consider crime prevention through environmental design:** This strategy uses design elements to reduce criminal behavior.

## Keep Yourself Safe while Pumping Gas

- **Stay aware:** Be mindful of your surroundings. Look out for any suspicious activity or people.
- **Keep the engine off:** Always turn off your vehicle before refueling to reduce the risk of sparks.
- **Avoid distractions:** Don't use your phone while pumping gas; it can distract you from what's happening around you.
- **Secure your valuables:** Keep your car doors locked and valuables out of sight to deter theft.
- **Use the night wisely:** If you're pumping gas at night, choose well-lit stations and park close to the pump.
- **Be cautious with strangers:** If someone approaches you, keep your distance and prioritize your safety.
- **Keep children close:** Always supervise children and pets, and keep them close to you while refueling.
- **Have your payment ready:** This helps you finish quickly and reduces the time spent at the pump.
- **Know the emergency procedures:** Familiarize yourself with the station's emergency shut-off and fire extinguisher locations.
- **Trust your instincts:** If something feels off, don't hesitate to leave and find another station or seek assistance.

By staying alert and following these tips, you can help ensure a safe experience while pumping gas.

## Safety Tips to Keep in Mind while in a Parking Lot

- **Stay alert:** Be aware of your surroundings, including people and vehicles. Avoid distractions like your phone.
- **Choose well-lit areas:** Park in well-lit spots to enhance visibility, especially at night. Avoid isolated areas.
- **Lock your car:** Always lock your doors and windows when leaving your vehicle, and keep valuables out of sight.
- **Don't be a soft target:** Be aware of your appearance as well as if you get distracted.
- **Be cautious while walking:** Watch for moving vehicles and use designated walkways whenever possible.
- **Look before you cross:** Look both ways before crossing any aisles, and make eye contact with drivers if possible.
- **Have your keys ready:** When returning to your car, have your keys in hand to minimize time spent at the vehicle.
- **Use your car alarm:** If your vehicle is equipped with an alarm, use it to deter potential thieves.
- **Know your surroundings:** Familiarize yourself with your parking area layout and remember where you parked.
- **If you are approached:** Use vehicles or shopping carts as obstacles.

- **Report suspicious activity:** If you see anything unusual or feel unsafe, report it to security or law enforcement.
- **Trust your instincts:** If something feels off, consider relocating your car or seeking help.

By following these tips, you can enhance your safety while using parking lots.

## Safety Tips: Protect Yourself while Going Out

- Always let someone know where you are, where you may go, and when you should return.
- Keep your cell phone on you and fully charged at all times.
- Go with people you know and trust. Date rape usually occurs when the suspect can isolate a victim.
- Be careful who you accept drinks from to avoid being drugged.
- If you drink alcohol, understand it inhibits your motor skills and cognitive understanding. Make sure you increase your efforts in avoiding dangerous situations.
- Never leave a drink unattended. NEVER.
- Do not accept a drink from anyone you would not "put your life into their hands." Remember, any stranger or casual acquaintance could be a suspect (even those people who are mixing or pouring drinks).
- If you are feeling sick or dizzy while out socially, go to someone you KNOW and TRUST. If there is no person,

you can talk to about your condition, call someone on the phone. Never leave alone. NEVER. (The intent of date rape drugs is to get you isolated and then to assault you.)

- If you think you have been drugged and cannot tell or call someone, call 911. A blood sample can be collected and appropriate tests will be run.
- Trust your instincts. If a situation or person makes you feel uncomfortable, leave. If necessary, call the police.
- No means no! No one has the right to violate your space or decision. Stand up for yourself and don't back down.
- Have fun and enjoy yourself, but be safety conscious. Choose your actions wisely and be responsible.
- Try to avoid using outside ATMs in unfamiliar or unsafe surroundings. If you must, be cautious about what is happening around you.
- Never drive intoxicated or with an intoxicated driver. Use a driving service or call a family member or friend.
- If you are using a service like Uber, Lyft, etc. Before you get in the car, check that license plate, driver photo, and driver name all match what's listed in the app. Uber rides can only be requested through the app, so never get in a car with a driver who claims to be with Uber and offers a ride. If you're riding alone, sit in the backseat. While en route, tap "Share status" in the app to share your driver's name, photo, license plate, and location with a friend or family member. They can track your trip and see your ETA without downloading the Uber app.

## Safety Tip: Protecting Yourself while Walking/Jogging

- Always be alert to your surroundings and the people around you. Walk assertively and at a steady pace.
- If wearing earbuds, make sure you can hear the traffic or people coming up behind you. Do not have your music so loud that you cannot hear your surroundings.
- You should scan the area with your eyes constantly.
- If possible, use the buddy system and go in groups.
- When on the street, walk/run facing oncoming traffic. A person walking with traffic can be followed, forced into a car, and abducted more easily than a person walking against traffic.
- Walk close to the curb or on the sidewalk. Avoid going close to vehicles, doorways, bushes, and alleys. When going around corners, make wide turns.
- Avoid secluded areas where there are few people.
- Be careful when people stop you for information. Always reply from a distance, and never get too close to the vehicle. Stay far enough away so you can turn and run if necessary.
- If you feel you are being followed, go to a well-populated area.
- Always carry a force magnifier—knife, pepper spray, etc.

- Trust your instinct. If a particular place, person, or situation makes you feel uneasy, go a different direction, and do not approach.

## Lighting

- Run during daylight hours if possible.
- Avoid dimly lit areas.
- Wear bright or reflective clothing.
- Consider carrying a flashlight.

## Companionship

- Run with a friend if possible.
- Most instances of assault on runners happen when a person is alone.

## Route

- Choose well-lit populated routes.
- Stay on the sidewalk or shoulder of a road.
- Run facing oncoming cars.
- Yield to vehicles at intersections.
- Only run through neighborhoods and parks and on trails known to be safe.
- Let someone know your route.

### Technology

- Bring your phone and use safety apps or share your route.
- Tell someone your intended route and when you plan to return.

### Identification

- Carry identification and emergency contact information.
- Make sure that your information is easily accessible and up-to-date.

## Safety Tips When Shopping

### *In-Store Shopping*

- **Stay aware:** Monitor your surroundings and be mindful of people nearby.
- **Secure your belongings:** Carry bags close to your body and keep valuables out of sight. Do not leave your bag in the cart unattended.
- **Use a shopping list:** This helps you stay focused and reduces the time spent wandering.
- **Avoid distractions:** Limit phone use while shopping to stay alert.
- **Shop during busy hours:** More people around can deter potential threats.
- **Park safely:** Choose well-lit areas and be aware of your surroundings when walking to your car.

### *Online Shopping*

- **Use secure websites:** Look for "https://" in the URL and a padlock icon.
- **Avoid public Wi-Fi:** Use a secure network when making purchases.
- **Monitor your accounts:** Regularly check bank statements for unauthorized transactions.
- **Use strong passwords:** Combine letters, numbers, and symbols, and change passwords regularly.
- **Be wary of deals that seem too good:** Research sellers and read reviews before purchasing.

### *General Tips*

- **Trust your instincts:** If something feels off, leave the area or situation.
- **Stay connected:** Let someone know where you'll be, especially if shopping alone.
- **Have an emergency plan:** Know how to contact local authorities or a nearby friend if needed.
- **Staying vigilant and prepared can help ensure a safer shopping experience!**

### *Don't Be Distracted*

When walking alone, day or night, it is important to be alert. Avoid getting distracted.

PUT THE SMARTPHONE DOWN.

A distracted person is an easy target. **Just put the phone away. Your calls/texts/email/social media can wait ten more minutes.** Messing with your phone means your eyes, mind, and hands are occupied.

## Safety Tips Pertaining to Your Car: Protecting Yourself in Your Vehicle and in a Parking Lot

- Keep your car in good working order and have the gas tank at least half full. Make a habit of filling up with gas during daylight hours. Never let it get so low you are forced to stop for fuel, particularly at night in an area unfamiliar to you.
- Leave immediately once in your car. Never loiter around texting, on social media, checking emails, etc. Being in a car limits your options and is a very confined space.
- When stopped in traffic, leave yourself enough distance (able to see the tires of the car in front of you) to make an escape.
- Park in well-lit areas and lock your doors. Check your surroundings before getting out of your car. If something is out of place or threatening, drive away.
- If an attacker gets into your car while you are in it, do everything you can to exit the vehicle. If you are forced to drive, steer your car into another vehicle, barricade, pole, wall, or any object that will create a minor

accident. While your attacker is distracted, escape and attract attention.

- If your car breaks down or your car is inoperative, use your cell phone to call for help and wait in your locked car.
- **Keep an emergency kit in your car:** First aid, tourniquet, flashlight, knife, paracord, and sharpie.
- **Keep a tool in your car if you need to break your window or cut your seatbelt.**
- **Stay alert:** Be aware of your surroundings, including people and vehicles. Avoid distractions like your phone.
- **Choose well-lit areas:** Park in well-lit spots to enhance visibility, especially at night.
- **Avoid isolated areas:** Don't put yourself in a position to be trapped.
- **Look around:** If you are concerned for any reason, simply walk past your car instead of getting in it.
- **Lock your car:** Always lock your doors and windows when leaving your vehicle, and keep valuables out of sight.
- **Lock your car: Always lock your car when you get in your vehicle.**
- **Have your cell phone nearby:** Have it fully charged and accessible.
- **Don't be a soft target:** Be aware of your appearance, and do not be distracted.

- **Have your keys ready:** When returning to your car, have your keys in hand to minimize time spent at the vehicle.
- **Use your car alarm:** If your vehicle is equipped with an alarm, use it to deter potential thieves.
- **Know your surroundings:** Familiarize yourself with your parking area layout and remember where you parked.
- **If you are approached:** Use vehicles or shopping carts as obstacles.
- **Report suspicious activity:** If you see anything unusual or feel unsafe, report it to security or law enforcement.
- **Trust your instincts:** If something feels off, consider relocating your car or seeking assistance.
- **Secure your belongings:** Carry bags close to your body and keep valuables out of sight.
- **Choose a safe location:** Research accommodations in safe neighborhoods.
- **Stay aware:** Keep an eye on your surroundings and be mindful of people nearby.
- **Know where the exits are located:** Know escape routes.
- **Avoid risky areas:** Stay clear of unsafe areas.
- **Relocate your car:** If you must stay out late, make sure you are parked close to your building. You may have to move your car after your lunch break, or before it gets dark.

- **Don't leave alone:** There is safety in numbers.
- **Carry a weapon:** Carry a knife, pepper spray, etc. Keep a tool in your car if you need to break your window or cut your seatbelt, or need to use as a weapon.

By following these tips, you can enhance your safety while in parking lots. By staying alert and planning ahead, you can enhance your safety while doing what you love!

## When Traveling

You can stay safe by being aware of your surroundings, being careful about what you drink and eat, and taking precautions to protect yourself from illness. You can also research your destination and get travel insurance. Staying safe while traveling involves preparation and awareness. Here are some tips to help you stay secure:

## Before You Go

- **Research your destination:** Learn about the local culture, laws, and safety concerns.
- **Keep copies of important documents:** Make photocopies of your passport, ID, and travel insurance.
- **Register with your embassy:** Let them know your travel plans, especially if you're going to a high-risk area.
- **Research:** Learn about your destination's customs, norms, and prohibited items.

- **Prepare:** Pack smart, get travel insurance, and check your passport's expiration date.

## During Travel

- **Stay aware of your surroundings:** Be mindful of your environment and avoid distractions like your phone.
- **Keep valuables secure:** Use a money belt or neck pouch to store important items and keep them hidden.
- **Blend in:** Dress like the locals to avoid drawing attention as a tourist.
- **Limit cash and cards:** Carry only what you need for the day and keep the rest secure.
- **Be aware:** Be aware of scams and don't accept food from strangers.
- **Be careful:** Be careful around animals and water, and protect yourself from the sun.
- **Be smart:** Drink responsibly, be careful about your money, and use travel locks.
- **Stay healthy:** Eat wisely, wash your hands, and avoid bug bites.
- **Stay connected:** Keep emergency numbers handy and have digital copies of important documents.

## In an Emergency

- **Know who to call:** Know the phone number for emergency services.
- **Get help:** If you need medical help, get it.

## Transportation Safety

- **Use reputable transportation:** Opt for licensed taxis or rideshare services instead of accepting rides from strangers.
- **Stay sober:** Keep your wits about you, especially in unfamiliar areas.

## Accommodation Safety

- **Choose a safe location:** Research accommodations in safe neighborhoods.
- **Lock doors and windows:** Always secure your room and use the hotel safe for valuables.
- **Familiarize yourself with exits:** Know the escape routes in case of an emergency.

## While Exploring

- **Travel in groups:** There's safety in numbers, so try to explore with others.
- **Avoid risky areas:** Steer clear of neighborhoods known for crime or unsafe behavior.

- **Trust your instincts:** If something feels off, leave the situation or area.

## Communication

- **Share your itinerary:** Let family or friends know your plans and check in regularly.
- **Keep a local SIM card or portable charger:** Stay connected for emergencies.

By staying alert and planning, you can enhance your safety while enjoying your travels!

Be aware! Be wary of public Wi-Fi. Keep your belongings close. Be mindful of your surroundings. Use your judgment to avoid unsafe situations.

## Have a Plan

- Make copies of important documents.
- Bring a personal safety alarm.
- Share your travel plans with a trusted contact.
- Consider using a GPS tracker.
- Download offline maps.

## Protect Your Belongings

- Secure your room keys, IDs, and other personal items.
- Lock windows and doors when inside your room.

- Avoid carrying or wearing anything expensive.
- Keep your cash safely.

## Safety Is All about Being Proactive and Prepared

- The more aware and prepared you are, the less likely you'll become an easy target.
- Always let someone know where you're going and when you should return.
- Identity the locations of the exits.

## Don't Be Distracted

Day or night, it is important to be alert. Don't be distracted.

Your eyes should be watching where you are going and scanning your surroundings. Being observant of your surroundings can help you identify potential problems before you're in the middle of them, and identify exit routes, safe places to duck into, and allies on the street.

Your hands should be free so you can defend yourself, or prepared for an immediate act like unlocking your car. For example: Before you leave the inside of the mall, locate your car keys. Have them ready in hand as you walk through the parking lot to your car. This way you are ready to get in your car immediately, rather than standing around in the parking lot distracted as you rummage through the clutter of your bag. Lock your car immediately after you sit down in it.

## Use of Force

Avoid any confrontation: The fight you always win is the one you were never in. Almost all attacks are avoidable if you do not become complacent to your surroundings.

For the use of force to be justifiable, it must be necessary and reasonable. The threat itself must be unavoidable and imminent. Justified force must stop once the threat ends.

Survival is always a fair game, no matter how dirty you play. Your attacker will not give you any advantage or dignity while attacking and violating you, so you must be willing to respond at that same level.

Martial arts can be an effective choice for everyone.

Some reasons why everyone should consider learning self-defense:

- **Personal safety:** Knowing self-defense techniques provides men and women with the means to protect themselves in potentially dangerous situations. Whether it's a late-night walk home, a solo travel adventure, or even just navigating everyday spaces, having the confidence to defend oneself can make all the difference.
- **Confidence boost:** Learning self-defense isn't just about physical techniques; it's also about mental strength and confidence. Knowing that you can protect yourself can boost self-esteem and empower you to assert boundaries in various aspects of life.
- **Prevention and awareness:** Self-defense training often includes lessons on situational awareness and risk assessment. People who undergo such training become

more attuned to their surroundings, recognizing potential threats before they escalate. This approach can help prevent dangerous situations from occurring in the first place.

*Don't be an easy target!*

*Be Prepared!*
*Improve your awareness and monitor your surroundings!*
*Evaluate your daily habits!*
*Avoid a potential threat!*

*Thank you for investing in yourself and your family.*

*Continue to Protect Your Assets!*

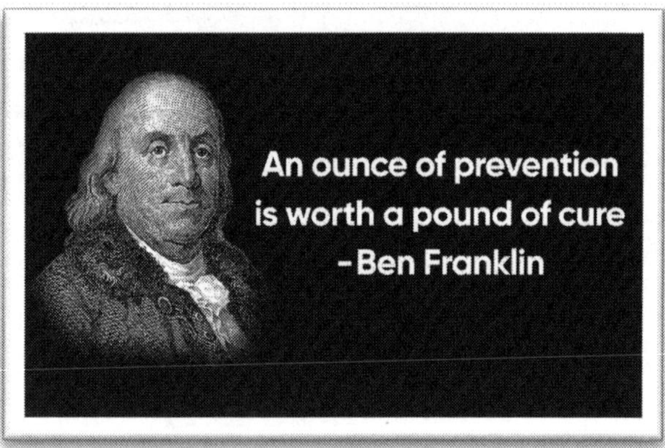

## Stay Safe

We really hope this book has provided some information that will help men and women out there feel confidently armed. We really encourage everyone to get some self-defense basics under your belt. Survival and being prepared should not only be a passion, it should be a lifestyle.

As a saying goes: "One must care for oneself before attempting to care for another." Practice the skills that will keep us safe and allow us to care for our clients and return safely to our families. Knowing how to react in any situation daily is absolutely priceless.

For massage therapists working in a private setting, personal safety can ultimately come down to physical training and the mindset to use it. This is the ultimate acknowledgment of personal responsibility for your own well-being. It is also the ultimate empowerment for your own peace of mind and self-confidence. Many therapists are reluctant to consider taking this step, but it doesn't need to be intimidating, and it doesn't require black-belt levels of mastery to be effective.

Be vigilant about safety. Learn how to help yourself and how to react to situations in a way that helps others.

We encourage you to share this information with your friends and family members.

## Training and Education

- **Self-defense classes:** Consider taking classes in martial arts or self-defense to learn additional techniques and gain confidence.

- **Legal workshops:** Some organizations offer workshops to help individuals understand the legalities surrounding self-defense.

## Resources

- **Books and videos:** There are many educational resources available that cover techniques and legal aspects.
- **Community programs:** Local community centers or organizations often offer self-defense classes.

If you wish to get a workout at home, a wave master is fun to punch and kick. You may be able to find one at stores that sell new or used sporting good equipment.

*This is a wave master*

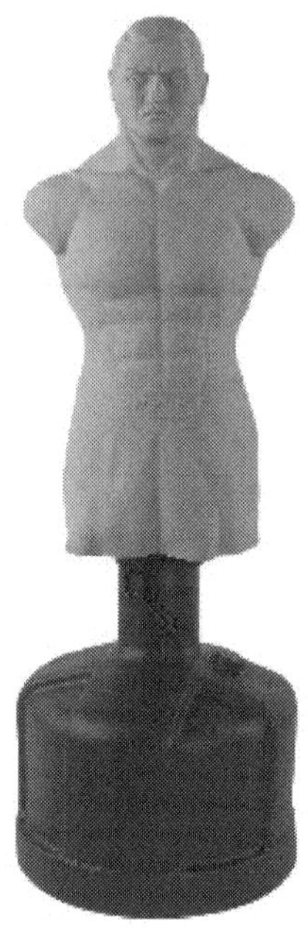

*It's a BOB for punching or kicking*

**Remember, the goal is to learn self-defense and NEVER have to use it!**

# About the Authors

Teresa has been a Licensed Massage Therapist for thirty years and Johnny has been a police officer for fifteen years and a Defensive Tactics Instructor. Teresa and Johnny are both Certified Personal Trainers. Together, they have developed a self-defense training program for massage therapists, other healthcare professionals, corporate teams, and teenagers to understand how to be aware and how to combat unwanted behavior.

Teresa has a BS in Health Sciences, is a National CE provider, World Champion Athlete in the sport of Arm Wrestling, and took part in the Movie "Over the Top" with Sylvester Stallone. Teresa is a third-degree Black Belt and has competed and won six Gold Medals in National Tae Kwon Do tournaments. Since the mid-90s, she has owned and operated a successful Massage School in Jacksonville, Florida.

Johnny has been a Police Officer for over fifteen years. Over the years, he has worked in corrections, patrol, various task force and specialty units. Besides his martial arts training in Jiu-jitsu and Karate, Johnny is a certified Defense Tactics Instructor.

With a lifetime of experience in the fitness and bodywork industry, Teresa and Johnny have created three fitness DVDs: *Practical Stretching*, *Strength Training with No Equipment*, and *Functional Strength Training with Resistant Band and Ball Exercises*.

Teresa continues serving her profession on a national level and has received many awards and recognitions. As a "Boston Marathon Finisher," she ran with Team Massage Therapy Foundation, raising $15,000 for Massage Therapy Research, and in 2019, she got inducted into the "World Massage Therapy Hall of Fame!"

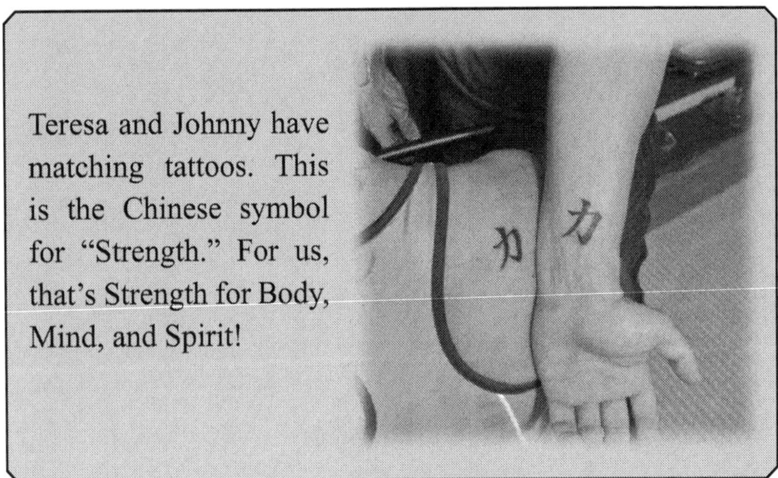


Teresa and Johnny have matching tattoos. This is the Chinese symbol for "Strength." For us, that's Strength for Body, Mind, and Spirit!

Teresa and Johnny love traveling and teaching their self-defense program to everyone!

If you are interested in hosting us for a private speaking engagement or workshop, please feel free to reach out to us.

We encourage you to practice self-care: eat healthy, strength train, and stretch daily (or as often as you can).

**Authors' Contact/Social Media Details:**

@TeresaMatthews10s
teresa.taglionematthews
www.HWFPTraining.us
HWFPTraining@gmail.com
SelfDefenseforMassage@gmail.com

Made in the USA
Columbia, SC
20 June 2025

59599776R00113